# THE ART OF SPIRITUAL WARFARE

A PRACTICAL GUIDE
FOR FAITH AND LIFE

# THE ART OF SPIRITUAL WARFARE

## A PRACTICAL GUIDE FOR FAITH AND LIFE

**REV. GERRY HARROW**
**COL. JOHN LEFFERS (RET.)**

TENTH POWER

**TENTHPOWER**PUBLISHING
www.tenthpowerpublishing.com

Copyright © 2023 by Spiritual Warfare Consulting
www.spiritualwarfareconsulting.com

All rights reserved. No part of this book may be reproduced without permission from the author, except by a reviewer quoting brief passages in a review; nor may any part of this book be reproduced, stored in a retrieval system or copied by mechanical photocopying, recording or other means without written permission from the author.

Scripture quotations marked ESV® are from the Holy Bible, English Standard Version®, copyright © 2001 by Crossway Bibles, a publishing ministry of Good News Publishers, Used by permission. All rights reserved.

Scripture quotations marked NIV® are from THE HOLY BIBLE, NEW INTERNATIONAL VERSION®, NIV® Copyright © 1973, 1978, 1984, 2011 by Biblica, Inc.® Used by permission. All rights reserved worldwide.

Scripture quotations marked MSG® are taken from *THE MESSAGE*, copyright © 1993, 2002, 2018 by Eugene H. Peterson. Used by permission of NavPress. All rights reserved. Represented by Tyndale House Publishers, Inc.

The views in this book are the opinions of the authors and do not represent the official policy and/or views of the United States (U.S.) Department of the Army, Department of Defense, or the U.S. Government.

King James Version, public domain

Cover and interior design by LTD2

Softcover ISBN 978-1-938840-56-2
e-book ISBN 978-1-938840-57-9

10 9 8 7 6 5 4 3 2 1

*To our Wives and to all our brothers and sisters
who are in the battle with us.*

# ACKNOWLEDGMENTS

We want to thank all those who made this book possible.

A special thank you goes to Elizabeth Giertz. This book wouldn't be what it is without her insights and tireless editing efforts.

We want to thank Rev. Michael Albrecht, Greg Finke, Angie Hinrichsen (LPC), Captain Kyle Hinrichsen (U.S. Army), Matt James, Rev. Dave Jung, Victoria Leffers, K.M.K. O'Day, Chaplain (CPT) Matt Mortenson (U.S. Army), and Vicar Ryan Pennington for their feedback, suggestions, and edits.

We would also like to thank the team at Tenth Power Publishing for guiding us through the complex process of publishing a book.

Above all, we would like to thank our Wives, Sara and Ann, for their unwavering love, encouragement, support, patience, and at times a kick in the behind to complete this book.

To God alone be the glory!

# TABLE OF CONTENTS

**Preface** ............................................................. 11
**Introduction** ..................................................... 13
**A Critical Starting Point** ................................... 17

    **Chapter 1** – Estimates ..................................... 23
    **Chapter 2** – Waging War ................................. 29
    **Chapter 3** – Offensive Strategy ........................ 37
    **Chapter 4** – Dispositions ................................. 47
    **Chapter 5** – Energy ......................................... 53
    **Chapter 6** – Weaknesses and Strengths ........... 61
    **Chapter 7** – Maneuver .................................... 69
    **Chapter 8** – The Nine Variables ....................... 75
    **Chapter 9** – Marches ...................................... 85
    **Chapter 10** – Terrain ...................................... 93
    **Chapter 11** – Nine Varieties of Ground ........... 101
    **Chapter 12** – Attack by Fire ............................ 111
    **Chapter 13** – Employment of Secret Agents .... 119
    **Chapter 14** – Epilogue .................................... 125
    **Appendix 1** – Bible Study Method .................. 131
    **Appendix 2** – Prayer Guide ............................. 137
    **Appendix 3** – Biblical Word Study on Satan and Demons ... 141
    **Appendix 4** – Advisory Staff Q & A ................. 145

**Sources** ........................................................... 147
**About the Authors** .......................................... 153
**Endnotes** ........................................................ 155

# PREFACE

The truth is, we are in a spiritual war that has already been won! As Jesus followers and God's chosen people, we receive our strength, the means, and the courage from Him to engage in battle. But as His people, we are also compelled to be as prepared as possible.

**"Behold, I am sending you out as sheep in the midst of wolves, so be wise as serpents and innocent as doves."** (Matthew 10:16, ESV)

In our different careers, we were both exposed to a powerful book, *The Art of War* by Sun Tzu. He was a Chinese military general and strategist who lived in the period of 771 to 256 BCE. Historians have devoted a significant amount of effort trying to discern exactly who Sun Tzu was, when he lived, and how this book of the thirteen chapters was compiled. The book was written prior to Jesus' birth and is currently being used by militaries across the globe in warfare strategy development and is widely recognized as *the* manual on strategy and tactics. U.S. Military academies cite *The Art of War* as a key text used to train officers in strategic and tactical planning. Marketing organizations also use it to help frame product campaigns against competition. In the book you are reading, the principles presented in *The Art of War* establish the framework to guide our study. It is our intent and hope to frame God's truths within the human concept of warfare to give us a greater understanding of how to better prepare and engage in *spiritual* warfare.

# INTRODUCTION

As a lay person and pastor, I (Pastor Gerry Harrow) have had real life experience with the realities of spiritual warfare. I've personally experienced health issues that could only be attributed to consequences from spiritual warfare in counseling sessions, have discerned spiritual presences, and have been used by God to help individuals heal from Satanic ritual abuse. This has led me to search for scripturally sound resources and preparation guides for people who find themselves in battles in the spiritual realm. What I've found is that the current cultural fascination with the spiritual world has led to a proliferation of material, but the sensational seems to have taken over and adulterated the truths found in God's Word. Scripturally sound, practical, wise guidance is elusive. You can find help, but for the most part, must sift through weak theology and doctrine to uncover the nuggets. Two powerful exceptions to this are the Concordia Publishing House publications, *Afraid* and *I Am Not Afraid* by Robert H. Bennett. Two additional resources you may want to add to your library are: *Grace Upon Grace, Spirituality for Today*, by John W. Kleinig and *Equipped, The Armor of God for Everyday Struggles*, by Christopher M. Kennedy.

I (John Leffers, Colonel Retired) served over 32 years in the United States Army, which includes my four years as a Cadet in the U.S. Military Academy at West Point. During my military service, I completed three combat tours of duty—each one a full year in length. My first two tours were in Iraq, and my third and final one was in Afghanistan. My job specialty was in the Infantry as a combat arms officer. Simply put, my job was to train and lead Soldiers to fight and win against our Nation's enemies in armed combat. It was dangerous but critical work. Failure was not an option, nor did we *ever* consider it even when at times the enemy seemed to have the upper hand. What kept us persevering was confidence in our training and equipment, trust in the wise decisions from our leaders, and above all a deep bond with our fellow Soldiers who we fought alongside day to day.

During my three years in combat, I became very familiar with my enemy's tactics. The lives of the Soldiers I led and my own absolutely depended on it. We studied the enemy's tactics prior to arriving in theater and continued to adjust our own based on the evolving threat. We always tried to stay ahead of the enemy instead of being reactionary. Unfortunately, we were not always successful and had some very difficult days. At times, we had to send our Fallen Comrades home to their devastated loved ones to bury or send our Wounded Warriors home to begin months or years of the physical and mental recovery from their wounds.

Over time the United States tactically defeated our enemies in Iraq and Afghanistan. However, there is considerable debate as to whether our overall strategy was successful in these two troubled countries. There was of course a heavy price in terms of the human and financial burdens our Nation endured. However, what I have come to realize in the last few years since I retired from the military is that we as a human race are fighting a much more sinister enemy—one that is not only hidden, but physically invisible in this dimension. This one is far more dangerous than the physical enemies I previously fought.

We wrote this book specifically for those who feel they are on the front line of spiritual warfare and want to be better prepared. Its purpose is to provide a biblically based, practical guide to prepare for, train, and engage in spiritual warfare. Throughout the course of this book, we will use military and historic examples to emphasize key aspects. It is designed to be a scripturally sound practical guide and is loosely written around the principles found in Sun Tzu's *The Art of War*. We have included real life examples of both spiritual warfare and actual military engagements to illuminate a point, practice, or principle. Our hope is that you will understand the realities of spiritual warfare, learn practices to prepare and protect yourself, and live as a person unafraid of this unseen warfare. We also hope you gain a healthy appreciation of its seriousness and the eternal consequences. In combat a warrior's physical life is at risk, but in fighting this enemy, a person's very spiritual (eternal) life is in grave jeopardy.

First, it must be said that if you're looking for a spiritual battle and think you will be able to do it on your own, you don't fully understand that this is God's battle. We would encourage you to put down your weapons and do some serious praying and studying! One thing is certain, if you don't fully rely on God alone for protection and strength, it will not end well. He is the one doing the work! You are His hands and feet in this battle... the foot soldiers so to speak. There are interesting examples in scripture.

**Then some of the itinerant Jewish exorcists undertook to invoke the name of the Lord Jesus over those who had evil spirits, saying, "I adjure you by the Jesus whom Paul proclaims." Seven sons of a Jewish high priest named Sceva were doing this. But the evil spirit answered them, "Jesus I know, and Paul I recognize, but who are you?" And the man in whom was the evil spirit leaped on them, mastered all of them and overpowered them, so that they fled out of that house naked and wounded. And this became known to all the residents of Ephesus, both Jews and Greeks. And fear fell upon them all, and the name of the Lord Jesus was extolled.** (Acts 19:13-17, ESV)

It's also important to note that even the disciples had difficulty with this.

**And when they came to the crowd, a man came up to him and, kneeling before him, said, "Lord, have mercy on my son, for he has seizures and he suffers terribly. For often he falls into the fire, and often into the water. And I brought him to your disciples, and they could not heal him." And Jesus answered, "O faithless and twisted generation, how long am I to be with you? How long am I to bear with you? Bring him here to me." And Jesus rebuked the demon, and it came out of him, and the boy was healed instantly. Then the disciples came to Jesus privately and said, "Why could we not cast it out?" He said to them, "Because of your little faith. For truly, I say to you, if you have faith like a grain of mustard seed, you will say to this mountain, 'Move from here to there,' and it will move, and nothing will be impossible for you."**
(Matthew 17:14-21, ESV)

Jesus attributed their failure to "little faith." And from whom do we get our faith? The Holy Spirit's work in us! Again, it is all God's work. He alone ultimately prepares us for battle and puts us where He needs us. He then provides what's needed to quell the enemies' efforts. You can trust in Him and have confidence that even though it looks like the enemy has the upper hand, God has already won.

So, what does spiritual warfare look like? That is a very important topic we'll be going into depth in this book. In this sensational world we live in, it is easy to think spiritual warfare is all about possessions, exorcisms, confronting the spirits, and everything that makes for good TV. However, as you read this book, you'll come to appreciate that it's much more subtle and dangerous because it's not as obvious. By the end of this book, our hope is that you will have ideas and insights on how to recognize and prepare for inevitable attacks.

We have talked about the importance of knowing who the enemy is and is not. The enemy is *not* other people or the government. The enemy is Satan, the temporary ruler of this world. The good news is that he can do only what God allows Him to do and that Jesus defeated the evil one on the cross and in the emptying of the tomb. Jesus' descent into hell was also a remarkable triumph. The bad news is that, from a worldly perspective, Satan can inflict horrific pain and chaos on this world. Read the book of Job if you want to see the extent to which he goes. So, on that premise, the people of this world who are not-yet-followers of Jesus are the evil one's prisoners. Locked up, tortured, with no hope and facing down death. But they don't even know it and are blind and deaf to the truth. They don't know there is forgiveness, life, and joy now and eternally in Christ. To keep them from hearing and experiencing the Gospel, the evil one goes after Jesus' followers. The enemy will try to distract, harass, and break you to neutralize your witness.

### Biblical Truths
1. The enemy is Satan, not other people, or the government.
2. He actively looks for victims.
3. God limits Satan's power.
4. Jesus won the war on the cross and in the tomb.
5. As God's people in this world, He protects, equips, and empowers us.

### Questions
1. What experiences have you had that might have been related to spiritual warfare?
2. What do you hope to gain by reading this book?

## A Critical Starting Point
### Victory in Christ's Power and Authority Alone

It is important to begin with a discussion of the whole concept of spiritual warfare and the implications for Jesus' followers. It doesn't take long to recognize that God's people are in an unseen spiritual battle. The devil and his demons are real, and he has the world in his power, but only as much power as God grants.

**We know that we are from God, and the whole world lies in the power of the evil one.** (1 John 5:19, ESV)

Possessions, oppression, sickness, and suicide are just a few of the consequences we attribute to Satan's relentless attacks on people. Scripture documents many instances of spiritual warfare affecting people's lives. Satan has been deeply wounded and eternally defeated but continues to create chaos and havoc in the lives of the people of this world. He has been ousted and dethroned by Christ but will use everything in his power to maintain his kingdom as long as he can. An individual who experienced demonic harassment and persecution powerfully captures the evil one's ways and purposes in the following poem (used by permission):

> Abuse- Satan
> It terrorizes your thoughts and dreams, day and night-
>    either past, present or future.
> It spares no one of whose lives it touches-
>    either directly or indirectly.
> It seeks to rob and destroy life-
>    either your own or those you love.
> Abuse- Satan's attacks
> It robs you of your self worth;
>       relationships;
>       faith.

Abuse- Satan's game
- It divides your soul;
  - those you love;
  - the truth.

Abuse- Satan's intent
- It separates you from yourself;
  - family;
  - friends'
  - God.

Abuse- Satan's delight
- It turns "me" into "they;"
  - Family and friends into enemies;
  - light into darkness.

Abuse- Effects
- It demands from those who love us:
  - Patience, when you're frustrated.
  - Sacrifice, when your needs are unmet.
  - Unconditional love, when you're vulnerable.
  - Forgiveness, when you're angry and hurt.
  - Faith, when you're weak.
  - Hope, when all seems lost.
- It demands from yourself:
  - Trust, instead of fear.
  - Love, instead of hate.
  - Truth, instead of lies.
  - Faith, instead of self-control.
  - Hope, instead of defeat.

Abuse- Healing
- JESUS brings Satan's defeat;
  - victory over darkness;
  - prevailing truth.

Blessings received and given are a committed friendship and love;

strong convictions and faith;
willingness to share and serve.

Abuse-healed memories.
Satan-defeated foe.
JESUS-Victorious Deliverer.

*K.M.K. O'Day* - July 1998

Coming to grips with the reality of this warfare can cause one to be fearful, cautious, suspicious, doubtful, and can even lead to lives not lived in the sure hope given in Christ. It can rob people of the complete fullness of life that God would have for His people. The result is a life of fear, timidity, and despair. If the battle is denied or ignored, there is also extreme peril. Many scriptures describe this battle and the devil's purpose–our demise.

**Be sober-minded; be watchful. Your adversary the devil prowls around like a roaring lion, seeking someone to devour.** (1 Peter 5:8, ESV) Ultimately, like all warfare, the consequences can be death, eternal death in this context. In Robert H. Bennett's book, *I Am Not Afraid*, he quotes an African Pastor who knew this well.

"How can you fight a war if you forget your enemies are hiding outside your camp in a bush? As soon as you walked outside you would be slaughtered." [1]

Bennet went on.

"Yet for far too many Christians this is how they proceed; they walk around without noticing the activities of the evil one in their midst and, as a result, fall prey to his affliction and death." [2]

Spiritual warfare is real, and many times the evil one uses difficulties in life to challenge our faith and belief. The reality is that we will continue to have difficulties. However, as God's people, we know God has defeated the devil through the work of His son, Jesus. God's adopted sons and daughters live in hope, know that God is faithful, and find comfort in the knowledge that nothing separates us from the love of God in Christ Jesus. That's great news!

**I have said these things to you, that in me you may have peace. In the world you will have tribulation. But take heart; I have overcome the world."** (John 16:33, ESV)

> But the Lord is faithful. He will establish you and guard you against the evil one. (2 Thessalonians 3:3, ESV)

> Who shall separate us from the love of Christ? Shall tribulation, or distress, or persecution, or famine, or nakedness, or danger, or sword? As it is written, "For your sake we are being killed all the day long; we are regarded as sheep to be slaughtered." No, in all these things we are more than conquerors through him who loved us. For I am sure that neither death nor life, nor angels nor rulers, nor things present nor things to come, nor powers, nor height nor depth, nor anything else in all creation, will be able to separate us from the love of God in Christ Jesus our Lord. (Romans 8:35-39, ESV)

Christ defeated sin, death, and the devil once and for all. His followers need not fear but rest in the assurance of new, eternal life in Him.

So how do we live in the hope we have in Christ while the battle rages all around us? How do we live knowing the devil has been defeated and we have eternal life in Christ? How can we find protection from the attacks of the devil? Scripture is replete with answers on all these fronts! One of the most well-known scriptures details the armor of God and how it helps us to stand firm.

> Put on the whole armor of God, that you may be able to stand against the schemes of the devil. For we do not wrestle against flesh and blood, but against the rulers, against the authorities, against the cosmic powers over this present darkness, against the spiritual forces of evil in the heavenly places. Therefore take up the whole armor of God, that you may be able to withstand in the evil day, and having done all, to stand firm. (Ephesians 6:11-13, ESV)

God gives us everything we need to stand firm! Truth, righteousness, the gospel of peace, faith, salvation, and the Word of God. He's also given us a way of life to withstand the evil one's attacks. Ephesians six goes on to encourage us to pray in the spirit, persevere, and stay alert. Martin Luther, a 16th century reformer, in his letter to Bernard Wurzelmann (1535), encouraged him to:

"Pray fervently and oppose Satan with your faith, no matter how stubbornly he resists."[3]

God has given us His Holy Spirit to guide and strengthen our faith. As God opens our eyes to His truth, He empowers us to engage in battle and follow Jesus.

Another simple but difficult truth to embrace is that our worldly assessment of our level of preparedness and strength is not a good measure. It's not about our strengths, weaknesses, or inadequacies, because God alone provides the victory!

> **The king is not saved by his great army;**
> **a warrior is not delivered by his great strength.**
> **The war horse is a false hope for salvation,**
> **and by its great might it cannot rescue.**
> **Behold, the eye of the Lord is on those who fear him,**
> **on those who hope in his steadfast love,**
> **that he may deliver their soul from death**
> **and keep them alive in famine.**
> **Our soul waits for the Lord;**
> **he is our help and our shield.**
> **For our heart is glad in him,**
> **because we trust in his holy name.**
> **Let your steadfast love, O Lord, be upon us,**
> **even as we hope in you.** (Psalm 33:16-22, ESV)

As the Holy Spirit continues to open our eyes to the truth and strengthens our faith, we experience the power of God's Word used in faith. Bennett captured this:

> **"Jesus' power over demons is ultimate and unlimited. His Word is the powerful and creative Word that, when spoken, creates a reality, the reality of healing, which is the defeat of Satan and his demons."**[4]

In *Volume One* of Dr. Jeffrey Gibbs' *Concordia Matthew Commentary*, he further emphasizes the power of God's Word.

> **"As the Gospel is proclaimed throughout the world, Jesus continues to drive back Satan and his forces."**[5]

God has given us all we need to withstand all the attacks of the evil one beginning with His powerful Word. In the name of Jesus even the demons tremble and are defeated.

Yes, all people are involved in a spiritual war, but in Christ your victory is assured. You are more than conquerors, and nothing can separate you from the love of Christ! Praise be to God!

**Biblical Truths**
1. Jesus has defeated sin, death, and the devil.
2. God is faithful.
3. We will continue to experience difficulties as Satan struggles to maintain power.
4. We are weak and unprepared on our own.
5. Nothing can separate us from the love of God.
6. God's Word is powerful.

**Questions**
1. What has convinced you that there is a spiritual war going on?
2. How have you resisted the attacks of the devil in the past?

**Tactics**
1. Keep a watchful eye for the works of the devil around you and depend on God's Word in battle.
2. Pray, study God's Word, and actively involve yourself in a strong Jesus-centered community.

## CHAPTER 1
# ESTIMATES

*"The field of battle is the place of life and death, the road to survival or ruin. It is mandatory that it be thoroughly studied."*[6] (Sun Tzu)

Sun Tzu further stated, "Therefore appraise it (War) in terms of the five fundamental factors and make comparisons... The first of these factors is moral influence; the second, weather; the third, terrain; the fourth, command; and the fifth, doctrine."

These factors are defined in the book as follows:

- Moral Influence or The Right Way: That which keeps their people in harmony with their leader
- Weather: The interaction of natural forces
- Terrain: Distances, whether the ground can be traversed easily or with difficulty
- Command: The general's qualities of wisdom, sincerity, humanity, courage, and strictness
- Doctrine: Organization, control, assignments, regulation, and provision

These words were written over 2,000 years ago, yet military leaders and strategists still study them throughout their careers. The military incorporates these simple principles in the way it plans for battle. However, the process is very in-depth given the complexities of modern warfare. It is beyond the scope of this book to go into detail, but we will describe the framework of the process in general terms below.

Prior to a major military operation, the military commander with the support of their staff conducts a detailed process to estimate how the terrain and weather will most likely affect friendly and enemy courses of action in impending battles. These estimates are at best educated guesses to help the commander formulate a strategy to defeat the enemy on the field of battle. When producing these estimates, there are two specific areas to consider–the area of operations and the area of interest.

The area of operations is the geographical area where the commander fights the battle. It is important to emphasize that the area of operations not only includes the physical ground but also the population with its culture, air space, and even cyber space.[7]

As part of defining the area of *operations*, the commander must also consider the area of *interest*. The area of interest is generally a geographical area that could have a positive or negative influence on the area of operations.[8] It is important to point out that the commander has the ability through the application of resources to affect an area of interest. A simple example of this may be an enemy missile base hundreds of miles away from a friendly force's area of operation. The commander must consider this threat. If the enemy deployed the missiles, it would be a major threat to their forces on the ground. In this example, the enemy missile base would be in the commander's area of interest.

In the context of spiritual warfare, the human race's area of *operations* is the physical world. The spiritual realm is in mankind's area of *interest* since the enemy originates and dwells in this domain. For an individual, this is the physical location where they work, reside, frequent, and travel. In the area of interest, a Jesus follower must also consider the areas that provide the biggest threats to their spiritual well-being. More importantly, individuals must also find and frequent places of shelter and "rest stations" with strong leaders and personnel to refresh and strengthen them. Healthy, Christ-centered, biblically formed churches, small groups, and parachurch ministries are the prime areas God has provided for these "rest stations."

Once the area of operations and area of interest are clearly defined and understood, the next step for a military commander is to understand how terrain and weather will influence military operations. There are two types of terrain to consider–key terrain and decisive terrain. Key terrain is usually a physical location in which the side that seizes or controls it gains a distinct advantage.[9] Decisive terrain is a subset of key terrain but is so important that the side who controls it stands a very good chance of winning the overall battle.[10]

In analyzing the terrain, the commander must consider both natural (e.g., rivers, lakes, mountains, etc.) and man-made features (e.g., cities, towns, tunnels, roads, etc.) and how they will affect their ability to conduct military operations. However, it is equally important for the commander to understand how the enemy can use the terrain.[11] There are prominent historical battlefield examples which illustrate that the force who used terrain more effectively was ultimately victorious. One prominent example is the Battle of Gettysburg at Gettysburg, Pennsylvania, on July 1-3, 1863. The Union Forces occupation of the high ground surrounding Gettysburg and General Meade's (Commanding General of the Federal Troops (Union)) strong defense prevented the Confederate victory over the course of the three-day battle. Many Civil War scholars attribute Meade's defeat of the attacking Confederate Forces (South) under General Robert E. Lee to his effective use of terrain.[12]

In the context of spiritual warfare, key terrain can be schools, workplaces, hospitals, social media, television, and radio. On the other hand, decisive terrain features are individual or family residences, neighborhoods, and Christ's churches. The Good News is that our Supreme Commander understands and controls the entire world. Even during the fiercest battle, we know the enemy can take key and decisive terrain only if God allows it. The other truth is God understands our needs as we live in key and decisive terrain as captured in Matthew six.

**And when you pray, do not heap up empty phrases as the Gentiles do, for they think that they will be heard for their many words. Do not be like them, for *your Father knows what you need before you ask him.*** (Matthew 6:7-8, ESV)

In any military operation, commanders must also consider the effects of weather. Extreme temperatures often adversely affect both the friendly and enemy equipment and personnel. Unexpected storms can turn dry roads to mud that makes them impassable for military vehicles. Dust storms and high winds can heavily influence flight operations for both friendly and enemy forces.

In spiritual warfare, the physical weather also plays a major role in the outcome of the battles. Severe acts of nature such as floods, earthquakes, hurricanes, wildfires, tornadoes, tsunamis, drought, and volcanoes have a significant impact on the will and faith of humankind. Victims of such acts will either draw closer to God or turn away even further. The enemy will use weather events to drive a wedge between an individual and God whenever there is opportunity to do so. Another way of considering "weather" is to assess the temperature and the direction of the winds of the culture. How fast is the world moving away from Biblical truths? From Jesus Himself? What is the general thought about Christianity? Where are storms brewing in the culture of the country? Key issues impacting our culture today include sexual morality, transgenderism in schools, abortion, racism, food insecurities, etc. They all contribute to the winds of the time and will be important factors in the outcome of the battle for key and critical terrain. Each issue challenges the hearer to assess truth from a biblical perspective. These issues will divide churches, families, and communities.

During this estimate process, the commander and individual Christ follower must formulate possible enemy courses of action to predict how the enemy may use the terrain and weather to gain a decisive advantage in the battle. In a sense, it is like a game of high stakes chess where the side that most accurately anticipates the opponent's move will be able to have its forces at the right place at the right time and ultimately be victorious.

Therefore, it is critically important for the military commander to put as much intellectual energy and effort as time allows in formulating their estimates. Once the battle begins, it is too late to conduct this process. The commander and their forces will live or die by how effectively they applied combat power based on the accuracy and completeness of the estimates. Thanks be to God that we do not have to figure all this out by ourselves! God has given us the Holy Spirit to guide and direct us. We are comforted in knowing that Jesus is in us and with us.

However, God's Word encourages us to do the work of estimating where and when the enemy will strike. To prepare for the battle we are in we must pray, be in God's Word, and stand our ground.

**I appeal to you, brothers, to watch out for those who cause divisions and create obstacles contrary to the doctrine that you have been taught; avoid them.** (Romans 16:17, ESV)

**Be sober-minded; be watchful. Your adversary the devil prowls around like a roaring lion, seeking someone to devour.** (1 Peter 5:8, ESV) However, the truth is that everyone in the physical world, whether they recognize it or not, is in a daily battle with the enemy. Therefore, it is important for each person to prayerfully conduct their own estimates. This will provide a significant advantage in laying the foundation required to successfully combat the enemy.

In the book of Nehemiah, God's servant, Nehemiah, utilizes the principle of estimation. He considered the situation, anticipated what his enemies would do, and took appropriate actions to protect the work.

**But when Sanballat and Tobiah and the Arabs and the Ammonites and the Ashdodites heard that the repairing of the walls of Jerusalem was going forward and that the breaches were beginning to be closed, they were very angry. And they all plotted together to come and fight against Jerusalem and to cause confusion in it. And we prayed to our God and set a guard as a protection against them day and night.** (Nehemiah 4:7, ESV)

**Biblical Truths**
1. The evil one uses his realm, the world, against God's people.
2. Satan can only do what God allows.
3. God knows what is coming.
4. God's Word provides counsel and wisdom. His sacraments provide strength and His real presence.

**Questions**
1. When have you underestimated the enemy's strength? What happened?
2. How can you be more observant and use that intelligence to stay in the battle?

**Tactics**
1. Prayerfully evaluate and assess where and with whom you spend your time (physical and mental). What areas of interest may be vulnerable and expose you to the evil one's attacks? Take one step to regain this area.
2. Stay informed of current trends, beliefs, political hot buttons, and cultural directions by digesting a diverse variety of news sources from both sides. Pray for discernment and wisdom. Compare findings with biblical truths and discern where it appears the enemy is making inroads.
3. Identify your resources and support networks.

## CHAPTER 2
# WAGING WAR

*"Victory is the main object of war"* (Sun Tzu)

Sun Tzu states that "victory is the main object of war." This principle seems obvious, but in real military terms it is often extremely difficult to achieve. There are countless examples over the course of human history where opposing forces have fought for many years before either side came close to declaring victory. One notable example is the U.S. conflict in Vietnam, better known as the Vietnam War. The United States fought this war as an ally with South Vietnam against North Vietnam. Although the U.S. began supporting South Vietnam in 1954, it deployed its first combat troops into South Vietnam in 1964 after North Vietnam invaded its neighbor to the South. The U.S. fought for over ten long years until a cease fire in 1975 and then the U.S. withdrew all its troops in that same year. Presidents Kennedy, Johnson, and Nixon initially involved and kept the U.S. in this region to stop the spread of communism from North Vietnam into South Vietnam and the rest of the Indo-Pacific.[13]

However, to Sun Tzu's point, the U.S. never fully prosecuted the fight at the strategic level to achieve victory. It merely hoped to deter and push North Vietnam back north, thus containing them. Moreover, President Johnson fought a limited war due to political pressures exerted by the U.S. populace, which prevented the U.S. Army from achieving total victory. Many historians have written on this long and bloody war over the last few decades, but in military circles, the belief is that the U.S. won every tactical engagement on the battlefield, but the political leadership lost the strategic fight and ultimately the war.[14] For one side to truly achieve victory, it must first bring its enemy to heel, and then that enemy must acknowledge defeat. However, when the other side does not acknowledge defeat and continues to fight, it makes total victory almost impossible. In the Vietnam War, the U.S. never brought North Vietnam to heel, nor did North Vietnam ever concede defeat.

To wage war and achieve total victory in the military context, a nation must be willing to commit tremendous resources in both human and monetary capital to fund equipment and supplies required to sustain its forces. It must be fully committed to the war and have complete support of the population that provides the needed resources. This was not the case with the United States in Vietnam. By the end of the war, the lack of U.S. citizens' support led to its strategic defeat.

Total commitment to victory may lead a nation to use any ways and means necessary to defeat its opponent. The government overseeing the military operations may choose not to follow the established Law of Armed Conflict (LOAC) agreed to in the Geneva Convention by many nations. It should be noted that the United States policy is to follow LOAC. Recently, the enemies the U.S. fought in Iraq and Afghanistan did not follow LOAC. The U.S. commanders and soldiers clearly understood this condition and factored it into how they conducted military operations.

Why is this relevant? In battle, it's important to understand and predict how your enemy will behave. We know that Satan does not follow God's law and plan. He will use any means he deems necessary to attempt to defeat God's people. Understanding this enables us to have no illusions that the evil one will try anything necessary. However, we know that God limits Satan, so we must depend solely on God's strength and provision.

Waging war comes down to three principles - commitment, perseverance, and tenacity. There are numerous historical examples that demonstrate the side exhibiting these three principles will ultimately be victorious. A great example is from the American Revolution. It took over eight long and brutal years for the young United States with far fewer resources to defeat a much larger foe. Although the colonists lost a majority of the battles, General George Washington recognized that to win the war he needed to outlast the British. His strategy was to keep his army in the field and prevent the British from destroying it. Over time, Washington's strategy was successful. King George III lost the British citizens' support and had to negotiate for peace.[15]

The Thirteen Colonies exhibited all three principles leading to their independence. They refused to quit, and the authors believe that God guided their quest to establish an independent nation. These principles are also important in Spiritual warfare.

There is only one acceptable outcome–total victory! Through faith, we know that total victory has been won through Christ on the cross. He gave it all, His very life, to completely vanquish the evil one and free us.

**He disarmed the rulers and authorities and put them to open shame, by triumphing over them in him.** (Colossians 2:15, ESV)
The rulers and authorities in this passage include demonic rulers and authorities, and Jesus defeated them all on the cross. In our creeds and in Scripture, we also see Jesus descending to hell to proclaim victory over those imprisoned there.

**"The descent into hell is part of Christ's exaltation because he fully uses his divine attributes and power. He is victorious over all his enemies. Even Satan and hell could not confine our Lord. He gives his victory to us."**[16]
What great comfort and hope that gives us... that the King of Kings and the Lord of Lords has defeated sin, death, and the devil and His victory is ours!

The evil one has been defeated but has not yet conceded. He continues to use guerilla warfare tactics against mankind. His only objective is to take as many human beings as possible down with him before Christ returns. Consequently, the evil one will use every lie and method of deceit to separate us from God and the eternal life Jesus won for us on the cross. We must be fully committed and relentless in this spiritual war, but the only way we achieve victory in the skirmishes is through our Lord Jesus. The question is, how do we do this when the evil one never fights fair, and we are unable to perceive his moves. As Soldiers of the Lord Jesus, He has given us the protective armor of God to keep us strong in His might and be able to stand against the attacks and schemes of our evil foe.

**Finally, be strong in the Lord and in the strength of his might. Put on the whole armor of God, that you may be able to stand against the**

> **schemes of the devil. For we do not wrestle against flesh and blood, but against the rulers, against the authorities, against the cosmic powers over this present darkness, against the spiritual forces of evil in the heavenly places. Therefore take up the whole armor of God, that you may be able to withstand in the evil day, and having done all, to stand firm. Stand therefore, having fastened on the belt of truth, and having put on the breastplate of righteousness, and, as shoes for your feet, having put on the readiness given by the gospel of peace. In all circumstances take up the shield of faith, with which you can extinguish all the flaming darts of the evil one; and take the helmet of salvation, and the sword of the Spirit, which is the word of God, praying at all times in the Spirit, with all prayer and supplication.** (Ephesians 6:10-18, ESV)

This passage emphasizes taking up the "whole armor of God." Just as in physical war, without the complete set of armor and weapons, we leave our unprotected parts exposed to the enemy. We risk losing the skirmishes and ultimately our life. When God's *whole* armor is used, our heart, mind, body, and soul are protected. Knowing that we are clothed in Christ's righteousness keeps us from the lure of works-righteousness. Understanding God's Word is the only source of truth helps us combat the cultural winds and gives us a biblical worldview. In faith, we know that we are covered by the blood of Jesus, that He dwells in and with us, and has given us the Holy Spirit. Knowing we are at peace with God because of Jesus gives us the urgency and boldness to bring the gospel to the world. Assurance of our salvation in Christ Jesus protects our thoughts and minds from slipping into despair over our sin. Shielding all of this is the faith God gives us through the Holy Spirit's work started at baptism. In faith, the evil one's attacks are extinguished! What a beautiful picture of our baptism! Roman shields were soaked in water before battle and would extinguish the flaming arrows when they hit. And our one offensive weapon, the Bible, helps us defeat the enemy with one word... Jesus!

In addition to the armor of God, God gives us His Word, a community of believers called the church, prayer, and "means of grace," including baptism and the Lord's Supper. Through these gifts, God equips us to combat Satan's lies, empowers us to stand firm, supports us in skirmishes, and strengthens our faith. It is critical that as Soldiers of Christ we don the *whole* armor of God and use the weapons Jesus provides us to defeat the devil. These are dynamic and effective tools if we use them. God's Word, the Bible, teaches us who God is and who we are in Him. The community of believers called the church provides encouragement, support, and battle buddies through life. Prayer is the way to communicate with God. The Lord's Supper and Baptism are tangible ways God has given us to experience forgiveness and His grace.

Unfortunately, there are casualties in every war. Sadly, many Soldiers lose their lives or are wounded in military action on the battlefield. The commander does their absolute best to achieve victory while minimizing the number of casualties in the process. Jesus' goal as our Commander is to bring us all into His eternal kingdom and rescue us from the grip of Satan.

**This is good, and it is pleasing in the sight of God our Savior, who desires all people to be saved and to come to the knowledge of the truth. For there is one God, and there is one mediator between God and men, the man Christ Jesus, who gave himself as a ransom for all, which is the testimony given at the proper time.** (1 Timothy 2:3-6, ESV)

In spiritual warfare, there have been and will be countless casualties. How do we know this? Because Jesus told his Disciples so when he was here on earth over 2,000 years ago. He stated that few would enter the Kingdom of Heaven. In other words, the ones who do not enter were and will be the casualties of the war with the evil one. However, physical death is not the measure. *Remember the devil's only mission is to keep us from eternal salvation with God–the ultimate defeat.* But our mission, the same as our Commander's, is that all people would come to saving faith in Him, that all would be redeemed and restored to our Father's Kingdom.

In contemporary times, we can see potential casualties of this spiritual war. It is a delicate balance to avoid becoming proud or presumptuous but at the same time recognize an inherent responsibility to call a fellow Christ follower to repentance and show the person the right path through Jesus. When you call a brother or sister to repentance, you should say something like, "I am saying this fully aware that the day is coming when I will need you to talk to me this same way."

**Brothers and sisters, if someone is caught in a sin, you who live by the Spirit should restore that person gently. But watch yourselves, or you also may be tempted.** (Galatians 6:1, NIV)

When we lovingly try to help that individual who is clearly on a path away from God, we are in a sense rescuing them from the evil one's grip. In fact, Jesus tells us that as His disciples it is our responsibility and duty to do so in His power. Conversely, as Christians we must also recognize when we deviate from the Word of our Lord Jesus and need to repent to avoid becoming casualties ourselves. As Christians we work with the Holy Spirit in maintaining our faith. The Spirit works through Bible study, worship, the Lord's Supper, and encouragement from brothers and sisters in the faith. When we start neglecting these gifts, our faith grows weaker, and our ability to resist temptations is lessened. The Bible warns that a person can even fall away from God and our faith. In Luke we hear about this.

**And the ones on the rock are those who, when they hear the word, receive it with joy. But these have no root; they believe for a while, and in time of testing fall away. And as for what fell among the thorns, they are those who hear, but as they go on their way they are choked by the cares and riches and pleasures of life, and their fruit does not mature.** (Luke 8:13-14 ESV)

It's important to understand that when you neglect your relationship with God and let Satan's lies occupy your heart and mind, you are spiritually in danger. The Good News is that no one is beyond God's reach. We have forgiveness and God's grace through Jesus. We pray that the Holy Spirit will keep us in our faith in Him.

It is critical as we live out our daily lives to recognize we are engaged in a spiritual war where the outcome has already been decided. We have total victory through our Lord Jesus and what we face are only skirmishes. It is a difficult and taxing fight, but we have the strongest victor in Jesus who will lead us to victory over sin, death, and the devil and bring us into eternal life with Him!

**Biblical Truths**
1. Jesus won the war on the cross.
2. God has given us the armor and weapons to win the skirmishes.
3. God calls us to bring the gospel to the prisoners of Satan.
4. People will either resist Jesus or rejoice that God has victory over sin, death, and the devil.

**Questions**
1. Which piece of armor gives you the most comfort and confidence at this point in your life? Why?
2. Where are the chinks in your armor? What armor has God given you that you've been neglecting?
3. Where in your life do you believe the evil one has gained ground and is winning the skirmish? What are some possible steps to retake that ground?
4. Who in your life is in spiritual danger? What are you being called to do to help them?

**Tactics**
1. Put on the whole armor of God each day. Read Ephesians 6:10-18 each morning before you go about your day. In earlier times it required someone to help because of the armor's weight. Visualize Jesus putting on your armor and remind yourself daily that Jesus won, and these are just skirmishes.
2. Make it a part of your disciplines to be in God's Word and worship each week to receive the means of grace. Pray continually and gather with fellow spiritual warriors for mutual encouragement and strengthening.

## CHAPTER 3
# OFFENSIVE STRATEGY

*"Thus, what is of extreme importance in war is to attack the enemy's strategy."*

*"Know the enemy and know yourself; in a hundred battles you will never be in peril. When you are ignorant of the enemy but know yourself, your chances of winning or losing are equal. If ignorant of your enemy and of yourself, you are certain in every battle to be in peril."* (Sun Tzu)

The devil is a master of strategy and tactics. He uses our weaknesses and our lack of knowledge of his tactics to try and take God's people down and to keep others from realizing their freedom in Christ. Sun Tzu highlights this in what he calls offensive strategy. In warfare there are two important aspects to this strategy– "know your enemy" and "know yourself." It is vitally important that we understand ourselves, specifically our weaknesses, strengths, and vulnerabilities. It is also important to know how cultural influences, pressures, and norms influence our day-to-day living. Additionally, we need to understand the unique giftedness and identity in Christ that God has given every one of his sons and daughters. When we understand our enemy and understand ourselves, "in a hundred battles you will never be in peril."

Sun Tzu states the following: "Thus, what is of extreme importance in war is to attack the enemy's strategy." But to attack the enemy's strategy, one needs to know and understand that strategy. Scripture emphasizes this.

> **Anyone whom you forgive, I also forgive. Indeed, what I have forgiven, if I have forgiven anything, has been for your sake in the presence of Christ, so that we would not be outwitted by Satan; for we are not ignorant of his designs.** (2 Corinthians 2:10-12, ESV)

Before an experienced military commander undertakes the dangerous task of engaging an enemy in mortal combat, they will first do what is called a center of gravity analysis for both friendly and enemy forces. What is a center of gravity? In the context of military operations, the center of gravity is the "the hub of all power and movement, on which all depends. That is the point against which all of our energies should be directed."[17] More simply put, it is the single most important capability without which either side would likely fail to achieve decisive victory.

An example of a center of gravity could be the support of the population of a nation sponsoring its armed forces and providing their strategic oversight in a war or armed conflict. For example, during the United States' combat operations during the Vietnam War, it won every tactical engagement with its overwhelming firepower and highly skilled Armed Forces. However, the U.S. ultimately had to pull out of the region when its population no longer supported the nation's strategic objectives. North Vietnam's long-term strategy to achieve ultimate victory was to prolong the war until it eroded the support of the U.S. population. It was ultimately successful.[18]

In the context of spiritual warfare, the evil one is in a bitter war with each follower of Jesus. It is critical that we conduct a center of gravity analysis for both us and our enemy. As human beings our relationship with and identity in Jesus is without a doubt our center of gravity. Without this precious identity, we have no hope and no chance of achieving victory over the evil one. Jesus defeated Satan when He died for our sins on the cross over two thousand years ago. Through Jesus' victory, He bought our salvation with His precious blood. We embrace the faith the Holy Spirit has given us and rejoice that He is indeed our Lord and Savior. He has redeemed us before God the Father and clothed us with His righteousness. Jesus is in us, and we are in Him. These Truths from God's Word are the only offensive weapons we need to disable the enemy's strategy of deception.

However, the evil one will viciously attack our center of gravity and work tirelessly to sever our relationship with Jesus. He will continually try to get us to forget our identity in Jesus, believe we must earn it all, and even cause us to question Jesus' ultimate authority in our lives. As a strategy, he uses our vulnerabilities and weaknesses to point out how miserably lost and unlovable we must be. In contrast, Satan uses our egos to lead us to falsely believe that we are the masters of our own destiny and can define truth for ourselves. The parable of the seeds sown on rocky ground is an example of Satan's tactics. God's Word is received with joy, but since it is not supported by Word and Sacrament, Satan comes and takes it away. A vulnerability is taken advantage of.

> **The sower sows the word. And these are the ones along the path, where the word is sown: when they hear, Satan immediately comes and takes away the word that is sown in them. And these are the ones sown on rocky ground: the ones who, when they hear the word, immediately receive it with joy.** (Mark 4:14-16, ESV)

Satan feeds on two more areas of vulnerability–selfishness and ego. The evil one understands he has lost the war, but he still wants to take as many souls with him as he can, so he tries every avenue to separate us from Jesus. The evil one will use the weaknesses and vulnerabilities that make us susceptible to temptation and sin. To anticipate Satan's attacks, it is important to know our vulnerabilities and those of our inner circle–spouse, friends, coworkers, and family members. The devil particularly targets vulnerabilities of self-image, security, and worthiness in many. Knowing vulnerabilities empowers us to preemptively employ weapons of protection and be on the offensive.

One of the means the evil one uses to obtain his ends is our cultural norms. Ask yourself if what you see on television, in your school either as a student or parent, or in your workplace is in accordance with God's will. There is only *one* normative Truth in this world and that is God's Holy Word as He speaks to us in the Bible. The evil one will not only leverage these un-Godly norms but will also look to establish new ones that go against God. The devil knows that if enough people accept these idols and even defend or celebrate them, then he can indirectly attack the will of Christians who are still fighting against these norms. It's even more pervasive than that. By making something that is against God's truths culturally or legally acceptable, he dulls the conscience of Jesus' followers and makes the unacceptable seem acceptable.

So how can we better understand weaknesses and vulnerabilities? There are many tools that can help. The first place to start your center of gravity analysis is with prayer and repentance. We know that even as followers of Christ we will still repeatedly sin, but God is faithful and forgives the sins of those who confess!

**If we confess our sins, he is faithful and just and will forgive us our sins and purify us from all unrighteousness.** (1 John 1:9, NIV)

It is important to daily remind ourselves that Jesus already paid for our sins on the cross. He bought us eternal life. The devil knows this, and he understands that his only path to victory is to completely sever our relationship with Jesus, who is our lifeline to eternal salvation. The evil one will do this by trying to keep us in a steady sinful state where we start believing we are not actually sinning and do not need to pray to our Lord Jesus or ask Him for forgiveness. If the evil one can accomplish this over the long term, he wins the war for our soul. Pray that God would open your eyes to areas of concern and strength for yourself and for those who stand with you.

One tool is the Christian Wellness Wheel. You can find it in *Vocation and Wellness* by John D. Eckrich, M.D. and in *Reclaiming the Joy in Ministry* by Darrell Zimmerman. Other favorites include *The State of My Soul Wheel* in Stephen Smith/Peter Ivey's book, *Solo, Creating Space with God* and the establishment of an Advisory Staff, a tool used by military commanders. We have also provided a list of resources at the end of the book.

The Christian Wellness Wheel is a tool that helps focus on the various aspects of our lives. It's a valuable visual aid because it has our identity in Christ as the center, a new creation in Christ, and is surrounded by our spiritual wellness.[19]

To use this, honestly assess your well-being in each area. Rate your wellness from one to five, five being very healthy. When you do this self-assessment, you will get a glimpse of your areas of vulnerability. For example, if you struggle with finances, Satan could use this to lead you to cheat or compromise your integrity for monetary gain. He could then try and convince you that it's okay because it's culturally acceptable. However, this would lead to guilt. Then, Satan could whisper in your ear that you're not worthy of God's love and ultimately drive you to retreat because of shame.

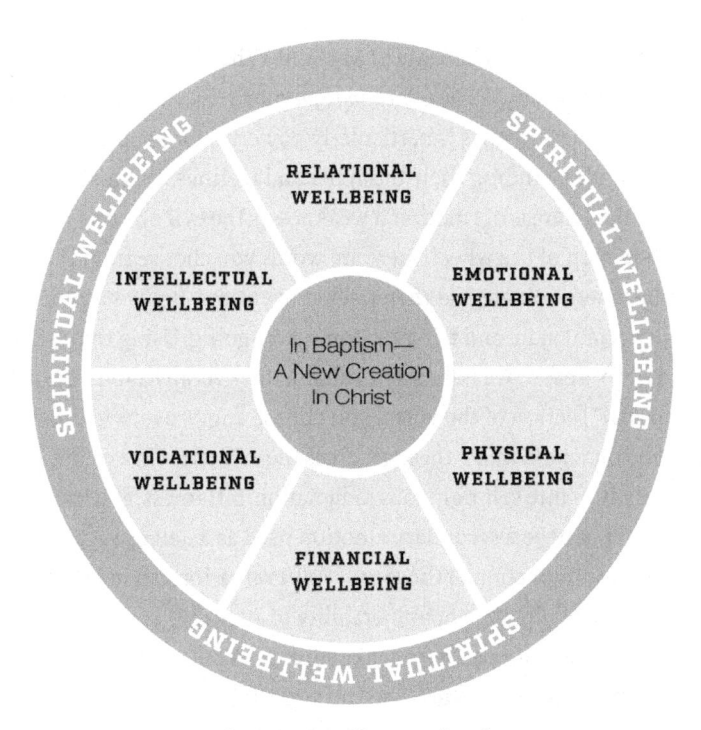

## Christian Wellness Wheel

(Wheel contents: Relational Wellbeing, Emotional Wellbeing, Physical Wellbeing, Financial Wellbeing, Vocational Wellbeing, Intellectual Wellbeing, surrounded by Spiritual Wellbeing; center: In Baptism—A New Creation In Christ)

Satan would then have you where he wanted you… alone, without support from brothers and sisters in Christ, and separated from God's Truths. Let's take another example. Your marriage or relationship is struggling. Since the world says it's not so bad to have other relationships or to turn to pornography, Satan tempts you with opportunities. You succumb, further destroying relationships and alienating you from God. Satan uses shame and condemnation to cut us off from the Commander and our friendly forces. Again… separated, alone, in darkness… right where Satan would have you. Remember what scripture says about him.

> **Be alert and of sober mind. Your enemy the devil prowls around like a roaring lion looking for someone to devour.**
> (1 Peter 5:8, NIV)

But God's Word restores a right relationship with Him by reminding us that there is no condemnation for those who are in Christ.

> **There is therefore now no condemnation for those who are in Christ Jesus.** (Romans 8:1, ESV)

The second tool, The State of My Soul Wheel, is found in Stephen Smith/Peter Ivey's book, *Solo, Creating Space with God*, www.solowithgod.com.[20] The wheel he uses is particularly powerful for people who struggle with understanding their thoughts and feelings. It is also good for understanding areas of emotional weaknesses the evil one will leverage. In each section of the wheel, there are words you choose from that help describe where you are and then track it over time. It gives a good view of your current state and the direction you're going. Using this can give insight into areas of weakness and vulnerability. As an example, if in the "Emotional" section of the wheel you choose angry, overwhelmed, and exposed you would know these are areas the evil one will exploit. Anger can easily turn into self-righteous indignation, bitterness, and lead to sin. Also, anger may be a secondary emotion used as a defense against fear, pain, or the anticipation of those two. Self-evaluation can help get to the root cause and help prevent vulnerability to attack.

Scripture encourages us to make sure anger doesn't lead to sin.

**In your anger do not sin** (Ephesians 4:26, NIV)

The third tool is to establish a personal Advisory Staff. This is not just an accountability group but is carefully assembled and led by you for wise counsel, encouragement, admonition, and friendship. The concept is to gather three to five brothers or sisters (dependent upon your gender) together monthly to share challenges and gain Godly counsel. The agenda is set by you and because you are a complete person, it includes time to share all areas of your life. The Wellness Wheel is a powerful guide to help in sharing. These times are especially helpful in areas needing attention and counsel. The Staff is made up of specific people tailored to give you the best, most realistic counsel. The power comes from being fully open and truthful as you share and answer all questions. It's equally important that the other members are willing to do the same.

In *Bounce: Living a Resilient Life* by Robert J. Wick, the author identifies the multiple voices needed in your life, and the people we would recommend for your Staff. The author calls them the prophet, the cheerleader, the harasser, and the guide. The prophet is the one who will bring truth into your life. They will challenge you to look at how you are living and speak truth into that. The cheerleader is the one who will give you unabashed, enthusiastic, unconditional acceptance no matter what. The third is the harasser. This person helps you laugh at yourself and not take life too seriously. They help you maintain and regain perspective. They are great at teasing you. Last is the guide. They don't take everything at face value and look for the nuances to help you discover the beliefs and outside influences that unconsciously guide your life. You'll be amazed how much cultural norms and influence impact your actions. It is also helpful to have men or women of all ages to bring a complete perspective. When done well, you will find this board to be one of the most powerful things you will ever experience. So, do it well! A caution... prayerfully choose the people you surround yourself with and be certain they are Godly individuals with strong, genuine faith in Jesus. Scripture cautions us against men or women in disguise.

**For such men are false apostles, deceitful workmen, disguising themselves as apostles of Christ. And no wonder, for even Satan disguises himself as an angel of light. So it is no surprise if his servants, also, disguise themselves as servants of righteousness. Their end will correspond to their deeds.**

(2 Corinthians 11:13-15, ESV)

You must implicitly trust the people you choose, and they must trust you. They also serve as your "battle buddies." In combat, a "battle buddy" provides strong support and friendship to the point that they would be willing to die for you. If you're concerned this may be too much to ask of your friends, the people who have been a part of our Advisory Staffs have shared that they grew more than they could have ever imagined. They too were better equipped for the battle through this process.

There are many other tools out there to support your center of gravity analysis. Find one that helps and then put it to practice. Once you identify an area of weakness, find and use tools that will help you be stronger in that area. Through prayer, discipline, fellow brothers/sisters, and God's strength and power, you will be better equipped to handle the devil's tactics and schemes.

We have discussed our center of gravity, but it is also important to examine the evil one's center of gravity. The evil one's center of gravity is like our center of gravity and revolves around a relationship with Jesus. He has been defeated and severed from a relationship with God. As much as our spiritual life depends on successfully protecting our relationship with Jesus, the devil's victory against each human being depends on severing that relationship. There is no other way he can achieve any other type of victory since it is impossible for the devil to defeat Jesus. Jesus clearly and decisively defeated death and the devil on the cross. This victory was complete, and it is final! Therefore, the devil's only chance for any type of victory is to win as many of the remaining skirmishes as he can against us here on earth. These skirmishes are the remaining battles that he has with each human being. The good news is that Jesus has provided us with the spiritual tools to achieve victory in these skirmishes. The devil's center of gravity, his tactics, are deception and lies.

> **You belong to your father, the devil, and you want to carry out your father's desires. He was a murderer from the beginning, not holding to the truth, for there is no truth in him. When he lies, he speaks his native language, for he is a liar and the father of lies.** (John 8:44, NIV)

> **You are a child of the devil and an enemy of everything that is right! You are full of all kinds of deceit and trickery. Will you never stop perverting the right ways of the Lord?** (Acts 13:10, NIV)

The most important thing we have in our life is our relationship with and our identity in Jesus, our center of gravity. We must proactively defend this relationship because it is our protective barrier against the evil one. Jesus won the spiritual war with the evil one for us, but for us to enjoy this gift, we must believe in Him! Through the faith He gives us and the assured hope we have in Jesus, there is no doubt that we will reap the fruits of His victory on the cross.

## Biblical Truths

1. The devil's strategy is to go after our weaknesses and vulnerabilities.
2. Christ died for us while we were still sinners.
3. God knows us better than we know ourselves.

## Questions

1. Are you more familiar with the devil's tactics or your own vulnerabilities? Why did you answer the way you did?

2. Which tool would help you the most in this season of your life?
3. What do you think are your weaknesses and vulnerabilities?
4. Is there a particular area in your life that seems to need the most attention?
5. Who might you ask to be on your personal Advisory Staff?

**Tactics**
1. Identify two of your top vulnerabilities.
2. Take one action for each to start strengthening your defense in that area.
3. Study the devil's strategy and tactics by searching scripture for every time he is mentioned. Use the word study found in the Appendix 3.
4. Create an Advisory Staff. For more info, see Appendix 4.

## CHAPTER 4
# DISPOSITIONS

*"Invincibility lies in the defence; the possibility of victory in the attack."* (Sun Tzu)

In sports and in warfare, it is said that "The best defense is a good offense." The truth is that our strength comes from God alone and that sinful human dependence on our own strength is inadequate and results in a life lived in fear and worry. As heirs to God's Kingdom and warriors in this world, strength and true invincibility come through acknowledging our sin driven weaknesses and our complete dependence on God. In God's Kingdom economy, the best defense is truly the best offense, and our defense is in Him alone. There are so many scriptures supporting this.

**The king is not saved by his great army;**
   **a warrior is not delivered by his great strength.**
**The war horse is a false hope for salvation,**
   **and by its great might it cannot rescue.** (Psalm 33:16-17, ESV)

**Some trust in chariots and some in horses,**
   **but we trust in the name of the Lord our God.**
(Psalm 20:7, ESV)

**For you equipped me with strength for the battle;**
   **you made those who rise against me sink under me.**
**You made my enemies turn their backs to me,**
   **and those who hated me I destroyed.** (Psalm 18:39-40, ESV)

> **I can do all things through him who strengthens me.**
> (Philippians 4:13, ESV)

> **Finally, be strong in the Lord and in the strength of his might.**
> (Ephesians 6:10, ESV)

So why is "disposition" important to our study of spiritual warfare? Let's start with what it is in a military context. The term "disposition" in a military context refers to how one army positions and arranges its forces in relation to its enemy. The object of each side is to achieve the best positioning and arrangement of its forces to ultimately win when the battle commences.[21] Below are several tenets that Sun Tzu discussed over 2,000 years ago regarding dispositions. They are still relevant in modern warfare and provide key insights into effective principles for engaging in spiritual warfare.

Sun Tzu stated the following: "Invincibility lies in the defence; the possibility of victory in the attack... One defends when his strength is inadequate; he attacks when it is abundant." He goes on to say:

- Anciently the skillful warriors first made themselves invincible and awaited the enemy's moment of vulnerability.
- Invincibility depends on one's self; the enemy's vulnerability on him.
- It follows that those skilled in war can make themselves invincible but cannot cause an enemy to be certainly vulnerable.
- Therefore, it is said that one may know how to win, but cannot necessarily do so.
- Invincibility lies in the defence; the possibility of victory in the attack. Stated another way, invincibility is defence and the ability to conquer is attack.
- One defends when his strength is adequate; he attacks when it is abundant.
- For he wins his victories without erring. 'Without erring' means that whatever he does insures his victory; he conquers an enemy already defeated.
- Therefore the skillful commander takes up a position in which he cannot be defeated and misses no opportunity to master his enemy.

- Thus a victorious army wins its victories before seeking battle; an army destined to defeat fights in the hope of winning.

Defensive actions are only meant to be temporary conditions. An effective army will only use them to gather strength in personnel and logistics to prepare for offensive operations. Logistics might include procuring weapons, ammunition, fuel, food, water, and other critical assets required to be successful in battle. In other words, the army generally does not have the capability while in the defense to go on the attack and conquer its enemy.

However, while an army builds up its strength in the defense, it also continues to study its enemy for vulnerabilities. Once an army has gathered the necessary assets to go on the offensive, it will attack the enemy at its weakest points to achieve its victory. There are countless examples of this throughout history. In military circles, the approach is known as the strategic offensive principle of war.[22]

During World War II, the U.S. was not fully prepared to execute offensive operations when it first entered the war after the Japanese attack on Pearl Harbor, Hawaii on December 7, 1941. Throughout the subsequent year of 1942, the United States remained largely on the defensive until it could build up all the personnel and equipment required to mount a full offensive against our enemies at the time, which were Germany, Italy, and Japan. The President and his senior military leaders correctly knew they could not conduct any significant major attacks until they had a military force that was fully manned, equipped, and trained, or they would not be victorious. During this build up, the U.S. military leaders also carefully studied their enemies' strengths and weaknesses to formulate a strategy to win the war both in the European and Pacific theaters of operation. Failure was not an option for the United States since the entire world balance of power was at stake.[23] It was truly good versus evil.

In the spiritual context, we continue to discover that our only source of strength comes from God, and that in our humanness, we need His constant defense because our strength alone is inadequate.

**How precious is your steadfast love, O God!**
**The children of mankind take refuge in the shadow of your wings.**
(Psalm 36:7, ESV)

Our invincibility comes through God's strength. We tap into that strength through repentance and total dependence on God. Recall that Sun Tzu stated, "Invincibility depends on oneself; the enemy's vulnerability on him." People can either have this spiritual defense in God or leave themselves vulnerable to the evil one's attacks. It is critical to clearly recognize and understand the failure to build a strong defense against evil puts an individual in grave danger that could cost their eternal life with God. The devil knows he lost the war because of Jesus' victory over sin, death, and the devil on the Cross and His resurrection. However, the evil one wants to prevent as many people as he can from enjoying the beautiful benefits believers enjoy in Christ.

We previously discussed that we must don our spiritual armor that comes from our faith in Jesus. There is no question that total victory belongs to Jesus. Given this incredible truth, and as believers in Christ, we know we are already victorious over the enemy based on faith in Jesus. However, in our human form we remain on the defense due to our sinfulness in the flesh. We simply do not have the strength or power on our own to defeat the evil one. We are utterly dependent on our Lord Jesus to lead us to our ultimate victory when we pass from this earth and join Him in God's Holy Kingdom.

Therefore, while we are in the defense, we build our strength against the evil one through prayer, reading scripture, the Lord's Supper, and repentance. By strengthening our relationship with Jesus, we erect an impenetrable defense against the enemy. Just like the U.S. gathered the necessary resources required to defeat its enemies in the Pacific Theater, each of us should strive to build our spiritual strength to fight off the devil in every skirmish. It is important to be "in the defense" with other mighty warriors. Part of the strength and effectiveness of a defensive position is who is fighting with you. Those you allow to stand watch with you make an impact. Therefore, it's important to be a part of a thriving church body that reminds its members of their defense in Christ. Together we are strengthened and can provide care for those who've been wounded.

This spiritual defense which again can only come through our relationship with Jesus also serves as a strong deterrent against satanic attacks. In a military context, an army would never mount an attack that it knows it cannot win. The evil one knows he cannot defeat an individual with a strong faith and relationship with Jesus. He may probe our defenses, but if we remain strong in Jesus, the devil will flee in search of a softer target when he realizes he has no chance of victory.

**Resist the Devil and he will flee from you.** (James 4:7, ESV)
It is critical that each person positions themselves in a strong spiritual relationship with Jesus through prayer, reading and reflection on Holy Scripture, and repentance when they fall short of obeying God's Law. This position results in an impenetrable defense that sets the conditions for Jesus to lead us on our final offensive movement from this earthly world into God's Everlasting Kingdom.

### Biblical Truths
1. It's in God alone we have our strength.
2. God provides all we need for an eternally effective defense.

### Questions
1. Why is it so hard to depend on God alone for protection?
2. What has helped you to realize/experience the protection and defense God has provided for you, His child?
3. What area of your life is the hardest for you to turn over to God?

### Tactics
1. Remind yourself daily through God's Word that worldly things will not last and are undependable. It's only in God's strength that you can live the full life He has planned for you.
2. Build a strong defense before the devil attacks.
3. When attacked, retreat into His protection and care... don't start depending on your own strengths.

## CHAPTER 5
# ENERGY

*"Now the resources of those skilled in the use of extraordinary forces are as infinite as the heavens and earth; as inexhaustible as the flow of the great rivers."*
*"When the strike of a hawk breaks the back of its prey, it is because of timing."* (Sun Tzu)

We are people of an extraordinary, omnipotent God who is inexhaustible and infinite. God's timing is always perfect, and He is all powerful. Our energy is best used to strengthen our dependence on God, follow the Holy Spirit's promptings, and increase our awareness of God's work around us. Jesus stated this so powerfully in response to the question "Which is the greatest commandment?"

**He answered, "'Love the Lord your God with all your heart and with all your soul and with all your strength and with all your mind'; and, 'Love your neighbor as yourself.'"** (Luke 10:27, NIV)

God works in each person's life, and we are to discern where God would have us engage. Sun Tzu's writings on "energy" reinforce this from a military perspective. It is important to understand that when Sun Tzu uses the term "energy" he is referring to 'force', 'influence', or 'authority'. Regardless of which of these terms we use, God is all three of these. He is absolute authority, an all-powerful force, and has unlimited influence on our world and each of our lives.

Sun Tzu stated, "That the Army is certain to sustain the enemy's attack without suffering defeat is due to operations of the extraordinary and the normal forces." In this context, he refers to a "normal force" as the part of the army that will make first contact with the enemy during an enemy attack. In combat, the "normal force" must first and foremost prevent the enemy from penetrating into the friendly formation and defeating its main body. Whereas the "extraordinary force" is that part of the army that will move to the enemy's weak points during its attack to penetrate their formation and defeat it.

Sun Tzu noted, "Generally, in battle, use the normal force to engage; use the extraordinary to win." An example of this was during World War II, when the Germans attacked the U.S. Forces in Belgium during the Battle of the Bulge in December of 1944. In this case, the 101st Airborne Division bore the brunt of the main attack, so they were the "normal force." Through incredible perseverance they stopped the German Army from penetrating into the main portion of the U.S. and Allied forces. General George Patton's 3rd Army, as the "extraordinary force", speedily raced to the battle to attack the German Forces at their points of weakness and ultimately pushed them back. This prevented a catastrophe during World War II.[24] Likewise, we must depend on our Lord Jesus to prevent a catastrophic victory of the evil one against each one of us.

In the context of our spiritual lives, we serve as the "normal force." With the strong aid of our Lord Jesus, our job is to become so dependent on God that the evil one cannot effectively penetrate our spiritual lives and tempt us to sever our relationship with God. Remember, the Lord is the absolute "extraordinary force" who has already defeated the devil through his death and resurrection on the cross. However, until that last day when He returns, He will continue to defeat the evil one on our behalf during these smaller skirmishes. He uses His "extraordinary force", His angels, to protect and cover for the "normal and extraordinary forces", His people. Scripture backs up this concept:

**...no harm will overtake you,**
   **no disaster will come near your tent.**
**For he will command his angels concerning you**
   **to guard you in all your ways;**
**they will lift you up in their hands,**

**so that you will not strike your foot against a stone.** (Psalm 91:10-12, NIV)

**Are not all angels ministering spirits sent to serve those who will inherit salvation?** (Hebrews 1:13-14, NIV)

Sun Tzu further emphasized, "Now the resources of those skilled in the use of extraordinary forces are as infinite as the heavens and earth; as inexhaustible as the flow of the great rivers." In a military context, he is referring to the ability of the combat leaders to have the expertise and understanding of the current tactical situation to maneuver their forces against the enemy's weakness to achieve victory. Spiritually, this is a perfect description of God's unlimited resources and ability as our "extraordinary force" to come to our assistance and protect us from the endless attacks of the evil one. We also know that the evil one is only given permission to do so much. When Satan went before God and asked to test Job's faith, God responded by limiting his reach.

**The Lord said to Satan, "Very well, then, everything he has is in your power, but on the man himself do not lay a finger." Then Satan went out from the presence of the Lord.** (Job 1:12, NIV)

God's authority thwarts and restrains what the evil one can do. He protects His people from devastation and defeat that would otherwise occur. Scripture promises that God will not give us any challenges or attacks we cannot withstand in His strength. Paul talks about this.

**But the Lord stood at my side and gave me strength, so that through me the message might be fully proclaimed and all the Gentiles might hear it. And I was delivered from the lion's mouth. The Lord will rescue me from every evil attack and will bring me safely to his heavenly kingdom. To him be glory for ever and ever. Amen.** (2 Timothy 4:17-18, NIV)

Great generals are the masters of their craft. There are numerous examples of such leaders throughout history. They understand how to apply their military resources at the right time and place on the battlefield to achieve victory. Moreover, they also understand how to position their "normal" and "extraordinary" forces to prevent their enemy from a successful attack. It is important to recognize that God is and always has been our greatest

General. He knows exactly how to guide and employ us against the attacks of evil one while skillfully maneuvering against our spiritual enemy to defeat him repeatedly.

**No temptation has overtaken you except what is common to mankind. And God is faithful; he will not let you be tempted beyond what you can bear. But when you are tempted, he will also provide a way out so that you can endure it.** (1 Corinthians 10:13, NIV)

What we also find is that He calls us to do our part in the battle to defeat the evil one's attacks against others. In one encounter with an individual who was experiencing satanic oppression, I (Pastor Gerry) was led to stand up, put both of my hands on their head, and pray for God's protection from evil. Days later, the individual shared that two powerful demons were restrained and repelled during that time, causing them great anger. In God's authority they were thwarted, and relief came to the individual unbeknownst to me. God calls each of us to listen to and obey the Chief Commander and engage in warfare regardless of our ability to see or even comprehend what is going on in the spiritual realm. The following is K.M.K.'s account of that day.

What did you do to my head today?

Again you placed your hand on my head-
> declaring us a child of God;
> confronting evil;
> willing to stand as that protector;
> signifying that we can trust you to journey with us.

But more importantly,
> that He is present and in control.

This hand of God that we experienced through you,
> kept us from running,
> from hurting ourselves.

This hand of God made us look at you,
> > listen to each of you,
> > trust each of you,
> > turn our head to continuously look at the altar and the cross.

This hand of God calmed our night thoughts,
> allowed us to sleep.'

> Your hand you obediently placed on my head
> represents God's hand and
> His power, strength and love.
> I can feel it at the time through you.
> I continue to feel it now through Him.
> So, what did you do to my head?
> You made us turn to and trust in Him-
> To help us experience His peace and healing in the midst of chaos,
> > in both the past and the present

There is no set play a good general can pull from their playbook and blindly apply to the tactical situation, because each set of circumstances is different. As discussed in previous chapters, the effects of terrain and weather coupled with the enemy's disposition will impact the decision making as a commander decides how to best employ the forces under their control. The key is for the general to understand precisely how much, when, and where to apply force on the battlefield to have success against the enemy. Again, our Lord alone has done this perfectly throughout the history of the world. He will continue to do so on our behalf because of His deep and unwavering love for each of us and for those who do not yet follow him.

If the general applies excessive force, they risk committing too much of their force and not having enough combat power to react if the enemy attacks from a different direction. If inadequate force is applied, then it may not be enough to achieve the tactical objectives against a well-entrenched enemy. God alone knows what is needed to protect His children or to convert someone to faith in Him and thereby defeat Satan's influence in that person's life. Once again, we will consider the Battle of the Bulge as a relevant military example of a general not applying enough military force against a well-entrenched enemy. During World War II, Germany launched its Ardennes Offensive, which was the last offensive operation the country was able to execute on the Western Front in 1944. The Battle of the Bulge, which is the better-known name of the battle, took place between the U.S. and Germany from December 16, 1944, to January 28, 1945. Germany launched its attack with diminished combat forces on December 16, 1944. They hoped to use the element of surprise to rapidly defeat the

U.S. combat units holding the line in this part of the Ardennes Forest located between Belgium and Luxembourg. However, through their tenacious defense, the U.S. Soldiers successfully repelled the major German attack. This prevented Germany from achieving its objective of a major victory that would force the Allied Powers to negotiate a peace settlement.[25]

In the military, this is called generalship, which is the ability of the general to make correct decisions with the information available and achieve victory against their opponent in combat. However, in spiritual warfare, good generalship is not enough to win a battle. We must rely on God as our one and only General and follow His commands and lead. Sun Tzu reinforces this by writing, "Order or disorder depends on organization; strength or weakness on dispositions." Once the general commits the forces to battle, it is imperative that the men and women in the force execute with more energy than the enemy. Lackluster fighting does not win against a determined enemy. Numerous historical examples highlight times when a general has made the wrong tactical decision, but the zeal of the forces overcame the misjudgment and carried the day.

During the Civil War, the Battle of Shiloh was fought in Hardin County Tennessee from April 6-7, 1862. General Ulysses S. Grant, commander of the Union Forces in the West, fought against the Confederate Forces under the command of the southern General Pierre G.T. Beauregard. On April 6th the Confederate Army attacked and seized the Union's southernmost camps. The attack caught Union Forces completely by surprise, and the Confederate advance forced Grant's Soldiers into defensive positions. However, after two days of hard fighting, the Union Forces under General Grant relentlessly counterattacked and forced a Confederate retreat.[26]

The same principle holds true in the daily war in our spiritual lives. The Lord guides us as the "normal force" against the evil one's strategies, but it is critical that we do our part to stand firm when the attack comes against us. The evil one is sneaky and the father of lies. We do not know when, where, or how he will strike in our lives. We must be vigilant and in constant prayer with the Lord, so when the attack does come, we will stand firm in our faith and continue to be His hands and feet. The Lord is the "extraordinary force" in our lives and will continue to protect us by defeating the attack of the evil one and open the way to further His Kingdom.

> **And pray that we may be delivered from wicked and evil people, for not everyone has faith. But the Lord is faithful, and he will strengthen you and protect you from the evil one. We have confidence in the Lord that you are doing and will continue to do the things we command.** (2 Thessalonians 3:2-3, NIV)

We would be remiss if we didn't speak of where we get our strength to stand firm. It's not a matter of being self-disciplined enough. Jesus sent us the Holy Spirit to guide, strengthen, and comfort us in the most vicious battles. The Holy Spirit is truly the "extraordinary force" we receive at baptism. It's in Him alone we can have the energy and strength to continue in the battle.

> **And Peter said to them, "Repent and be baptized every one of you in the name of Jesus Christ for the forgiveness of your sins, and you will receive the gift of the Holy Spirit."** (Acts 2:38, ESV)

> **But the Helper, the Holy Spirit, whom the Father will send in my name, he will teach you all things and bring to your remembrance all that I have said to you.** (John 14:26, ESV)

> **But you will receive power when the Holy Spirit has come upon you, and you will be my witnesses in Jerusalem and in all Judea and Samaria, and to the end of the earth.** (Acts 1:8, ESV)

### Biblical Truths

1. God gave us the Holy Spirit to guide, comfort, and strengthen us for the battle.
2. God establishes boundaries to what Satan can do in the war.
3. There is a spiritual army, God's angels, that carries on in the unseen battle.

### Questions

1. What part of this chapter is the hardest for you to comprehend?

2. What's your go-to source of "energy" when you find yourself tempted, attacked, and under siege?
3. What's your reaction to seeing God as the Great General directing the war here on earth?

**Tactics**

1. Remind yourself daily of your baptism and the gift of the Holy Spirit. As an example, when you wash your face, remind yourself that your identity is in Christ, that you are a beloved child of God, and He is with you.
2. Daily spend time in God's Word, solitude (alone without distractions), and quietness to be in God's presence.
3. Watch and note extraordinary occurrences of God's intervention in your life.

CHAPTER 6

# WEAKNESSES AND STRENGTHS

> *"If I am able to determine the enemy's dispositions while at the same time I conceal my own then I can concentrate and he must divide."* (Sun Tzu)
> *"Now an army may be likened to water, for just as flowing water avoids the heights and hastens to the lowlands, so an army avoids strength and strikes weaknesses."* (Sun Tzu)

One of the best tactics in spiritual warfare is to avoid the enemy's strongholds and depend on an effective defense against the evil one's relentless attacks. A two-fold approach includes discerning what God is calling us to do in our lives and bivouacking in God, our refuge and fortress.

One of the major tenets that Sun Tzu makes over 2,000 years ago is, "Now an army may be likened to water, for just as flowing water avoids the heights and hastens to the lowlands, so an army avoids strength and strikes weaknesses."

In the military, a commander must always conduct a reconnaissance of their enemy to identify its weaknesses before blindly launching an attack that risks losing their force. The military commander can then formulate a plan to exploit those weaknesses and achieve victory. A successful commander also knows they must protect their own points of vulnerability from the enemy or risk having an attack penetrate those weak points and thus lose their force. During combat operations, it is a brutal back and forth where each side constantly seeks to hide and protect its vulnerabilities from its respective foe while at the same time always seeking an opportunity to identify its enemy's weakness. Each side fervently seeks the other's most vulnerable point, so it can attack to exploit that weakness and ultimately gain victory.

In the Spiritual context, each individual whether he or she knows it or not, is at constant war with the evil one. Like opposing military forces in combat, the evil one is always looking to identify our weakness and then attack that vulnerability to achieve victory over us.

**Be sober-minded; be watchful. Your adversary the devil prowls around like a roaring lion, seeking someone to devour.** (1 Peter 5:8, ESV)

These attacks may not be blatant but are often rather subtle, so that an individual may not even realize that they are under attack. This is one of the reasons the evil one is so sinister. As humans we have many weaknesses the evil one can find and exploit. We've discussed this extensively in Chapter 4 and reiterate that they can include addictions, strong desires for money or power, sexual immorality, pride or self-loathing, and even indifference to or unbelief in God. A logical question that you may ask after reading this passage is, what is the evil one's weakness and how we can exploit it in our spiritual war? One of the Devil's weaknesses is his ego. Martin Luther captured this well.

"For the devil is an exceptionally arrogant spirit, together with the world, his bride... when he sees that we are resolved to hold out against all his hatred, anger, and trouble, hold out in high spirits at that, and continue on our way just to spite him, then he is the first to tire; for his arrogance is so great that he is unable to bear any defiance and contempt."[27]

But ultimately, the evil one's weakness is God's Truth. He hates the Truth. God's Truth is that the Father sent His only Son to save weak, sinful, undeserving people like you and me.

**...but God shows his love for us in that while we were still sinners, Christ died for us.** (Romans 5:8, ESV)

Our Lord Jesus became incarnate (human with flesh and blood), was crucified, and died on the Cross for our sins. When Jesus died on the Cross for us as a blood sacrifice to atone for all of mankind's sins, past, present, and future, before God the Father, and then was resurrected three days later, he saved each one of us from death. Moreover, through faith in Christ, He not only saved us from death but also promised us eternal life with our Lord in Heaven. This is good news! But it is Satan's weakness.

The evil one does not think this is such good news and will work tirelessly to distract or prevent us from seeking and embracing God's Truth. For Satan knows that once we live in our God given faith, truly internalize God's Truths, and place our treasures not on things in this physical world but rather on our faith in Jesus, there are no points of vulnerability he can successfully attack. Moreover, the evil one knows he cannot successfully attack Jesus. Jesus is *all* powerful and defeated Satan permanently when He died for us on the Cross and freed all believers from death and eternal damnation. When we cling to Jesus and use Him as our impenetrable spiritual shield, we have no points of weakness for the devil to attack.

**The Lord is my rock and my fortress and my deliverer, my God, my rock, in whom I take refuge, my shield, and the horn of my salvation, my stronghold.** (Psalm 18:2, ESV)

**God is our refuge and strength, a very present help in trouble.** (Psalm 46:1, ESV)

**Trust in him at all times, O people; pour out your heart before him; God is a refuge for us.** (Psalm 62:8, ESV)

However, on the flip side, if we allow the evil one to identify and exploit one of our weaknesses because we drift away from our faith or get lax in our relationship with Jesus, we open ourselves up for the possibility of a successful attack against us. It is important to remember that Satan knows he can no longer win the war against God; however, he still wants to take as many of us into the depths of hell with him when he is finally bound by our Lord Jesus when He comes again. From a practical perspective, there have been many people who have put themselves in harm's way who find themselves walking into a Pastor's office for counseling. They have not purposefully resisted Satan's areas of strength and have frequented places like bars and pornography sources. They have skirted danger with "innocent" flirtations, inappropriate jokes and language, and many other activities deemed okay because the culture says it's acceptable. Many have said that they didn't intend for it to go as far as it did, but they got caught up in the moment. The evil one lured them into an ambush! He uses money, sex, and power as His primary areas of strength. Scripture encourages us to be wary, stay away, and live lives worthy of our calling.

> **Therefore, if anyone cleanses himself from what is dishonorable, he will be a vessel for honorable use, set apart as holy, useful to the master of the house, ready for every good work. So flee youthful passions and pursue righteousness, faith, love, and peace, along with those who call on the Lord from a pure heart. Have nothing to do with foolish, ignorant controversies; you know that they breed quarrels.** (2 Timothy 2:21-23, ESV)

In Matthew 4 and Luke 4, we read how Satan tempted Jesus in every way. But Jesus used God's Word to resist everything he threw at Him. It is critical that each one of us continues to protect our faith and resists putting ourselves into Satan's areas of strength. This helps prevent the evil one from penetrating our points of weakness. God's Word promises that God is faithful, and He will save and train us. Knowing Jesus has already defeated Satan provides a great source of comfort and strength for His followers.

> **Submit yourselves therefore to God. Resist the devil, and he will flee from you.** (James 4:7, ESV)

> **No temptation has overtaken you that is not common to man. God is faithful, and he will not let you be tempted beyond your ability, but with the temptation he will also provide the way of escape, that you may be able to endure it.** (1 Corinthians 10:13, ESV)

> **Watch and pray that you may not enter into temptation. The spirit indeed is willing, but the flesh is weak."** (Matthew 26:41, ESV)

> **Blessed be the Lord, my rock, who trains my hands for war, and my fingers for battle;** (Psalm 144:1, ESV)

Sun Tzu states: "Therefore, against those skilled in attack, an enemy does not know where to defend; against the experts in defense, the enemy does not know where to attack." If we use the second part of this quote and apply it to our spiritual lives, we must become "experts in defense" by building and maintaining, through the Holy Spirit's work in us, a strong faith in Jesus. It can take days, weeks, months, and sometimes even years for a military force to accomplish all the complex tasks required to build a strong defense. Soldiers will use earth works, concertina and barbed wire, tank ditches, mines, and heavy artillery and machine gun emplacements that are carefully positioned to successfully thwart the enemy's inevitable attack.

We see an example of a successful defense during the Korean War when a U.S. Infantry Regiment along with French Forces consisting of about 4,500 soldiers prevented three Chinese divisions of roughly 3,000-5,000 soldiers from seizing the key terrain of Chipyong-ni located about 35 miles east of Seoul, Korea. Of note, Seoul is the capital of South Korea and was a major objective of the Chinese, our enemy at the time. The battle lasted three days and three nights, but after bitter fighting, the U.S. and French forces emerged victorious taking light casualties. However, the Chinese Communist Forces (CCF) lost about a third of their soldiers. This important battle thwarted the CCF's momentum, and many historians believe it allowed the U.S. to prevent the entire Korean Peninsula from falling into Chinese communist hands.[28]

Spiritually, erecting a strong defense against attacks from the evil one in the same way the U.S. did at the Battle of Chipyong-ni against the CCF may take several years to build, maintain, and fortify. The first step as discussed before is knowing our vulnerabilities and areas of weakness. For our part in building a successful spiritual defense we:
- Pray to maintain and build our relationship with God.
- Study God's Holy and infallible Word.
- Attend worship frequently to strengthen our spiritual lives.
- Fellowship with our brothers and sisters in Christ to support each other.
- Receive the sacrament of Holy Communion to be fed by God.
- Examine ourselves, repent of our sins, and receive His forgiveness.

These are not one-time events, but rather, we take great pleasure in repeating them over and over. The Holy Spirit works in us through these disciplines. We can be joyful in our faith in our Lord Jesus and grateful to Him that He is our only true defense against the vicious and relentless attacks by the evil one. He *is* our spiritual protection, our refuge, and fortress!

It is imperative that we build as strong a spiritual defense as possible, because as humans it is impossible to hide all our vulnerabilities from the evil one. This is because we are inherently sinful by nature. The good news, however, is that Jesus is our shield of armor, and even though we are unable to conceal our vulnerabilities, our Lord has forgiven all our sins through His sacrifice on the cross. Therefore, the evil one has no sway over us. Jesus is our shield of armor whose protection never fails or wavers, and we give Him thanks, praise, and honor for His faithfulness. It's because of Christ alone that we have a strong defense. He alone equips and strengthens us to avoid Satan's temptations and areas of strength. Be encouraged through God's Word in Titus.

> For the grace of God has appeared, bringing salvation for all people, training us to renounce ungodliness and worldly passions, and to live self-controlled, upright, and godly lives in the present age, waiting for our blessed hope, the appearing of the glory of our great God and Savior Jesus Christ, who gave himself for us to redeem us from all lawlessness and to purify for himself a people for his own possession who are zealous for good works. (Titus 2:11-14, ESV)

The next time you feel accused by the devil, you might want to take some advice from Martin Luther:

"Jesus Christ certainly did not inspire the thought that the devil will get you; for He died in order that those who belong to the devil might be free from him. Therefore act like this: Spit at the devil and say: If I have sinned, well, then I have sinned, and I am sorry about it; but Christ has taken away all the sins of all the world if only people will confess them, do better, and believe in Christ. Therefore this sin of mine is certainly also taken away. Depart from me, devil. I am absolved."[29]

## Biblical Truths

1. God is our fortress and refuge.
2. Satan will tempt us with many worldly enticements.
3. God alone gives us the strength to resist and live holy lives for Him.

**Questions:**
1. What temptation is the most difficult for you? Where do you encounter it the most?
2. Which areas of your defense (prayer, God's Word, worship, fellowship, the Lord's Supper, repentance, and forgiveness) have you neglected?
3. Where are your vulnerabilities and where are the evil one's strongholds in your life? Read about Jesus' temptation as recounted in Matthew 4 and Luke 4. Ask yourself the question... How does this inform my encounters with temptation? What can I learn from Jesus?

**Tactics**
1. Pick one of your vulnerabilities or areas you may have neglected. After prayer, develop and implement a plan to improve in this area. Remember to build in accountability.
2. Memorize at least two of the Scripture passages from this chapter:
   1 Peter 5:8, Romans 5:8, Psalm 18:2, Psalm 46:1, Psalm 62:8, 2 Timothy 2:21-23, James 4:7, 1 Corinthians 10:13, Matthew 26:41, Psalm 144:1, Titus 2:11-14

## CHAPTER 7
# MANEUVER

*"Weigh the situation, then move."* (Sun Tzu)

Modern culture values action. Unfortunately, many of us jump into action before we understand the magnitude and implications. This habit often creates less than desired results. In my (Gerry) engineering work, we had a pump that wasn't performing, and the mechanics assumed the pump was the problem. They replaced it but, after much expense and effort, the problem continued. After stepping back, analyzing, and weighing the situation, we installed a vortex preventer in the bottom of the tank. It solved the issue. It was a much cheaper solution, and it fixed the problem.

Too many times in our lives, we move and make decisions before weighing the situation. This can be disastrous in warfare, particularly true in spiritual warfare. The good news is that there are tools you can use to "weigh" a situation before engaging. These entail prayer, silence, solitude, and seeking wise counsel. Sun Tzu knew the importance in military operations and in this chapter, you'll see its relevance in spiritual warfare. Sun Tzu stated, "Weigh the situation, then move." It's important to pause, consider the situation and then move. Too often we rush in and find ourselves in a much different scenario than we first thought, resulting in disaster.

*"Normally when the army is employed, the general first receives his commands from the sovereign. He assembles the troops and mobilizes the people. He blends the army into a harmonious entity and encamps it."* (Sun Tzu)

In the military context, high level U.S. Military commanders receive campaign guidance and subsequent orders directly from the President of the

United States, our "sovereign" civic leader. Once the general receives their orders, they will issue the appropriate commands to subordinate military officers and noncommissioned officers to assemble and position the troops to prepare for combat operations.

In the spiritual context, as Christians we receive our guidance from our Lord Jesus through the Holy Spirit. Jesus is our supreme "sovereign" whose authority surpasses all others. His commands come to us directly through God's Word, discerned through prayer, and the work of the Holy Spirit. Through constant prayer and reading of Scripture, it is possible to hear and embrace our Lord's commands and desires for our lives. His Word provides us guidance for how we should conduct ourselves in our daily lives. The Holy Spirit leads, teaches and strengthens us on the journey. God's Word shows how to remain in God's grace and helps us maintain a strong spiritual armor to thwart the attacks from the evil one.

**Plans are established by counsel; by wise guidance wage war.**
(Proverbs 20:18, ESV)

Sun Tzu continues: "Nothing is more difficult than the art of maneuver. What is difficult about maneuver is to make the devious route the most direct and to turn misfortune to advantage." In military terms, maneuver refers to an army conducting fire and movement to place itself in a position of relative advantage to the enemy.[30] A seasoned general clearly understands that their best chance to defeat the enemy is to outmaneuver the enemy while ensuring that this same enemy does not outmaneuver their own army.

An excellent example of this in history is during the Korean War when General Douglas McArthur conducted the Inchon Landing from September 10-19, 1950. During this campaign he landed the U.S. Army through amphibious operations (troop movement by the sea) behind the North Korean enemy force at the time. This turned the tide of the war. The U.S. had been losing at this point but was able to regain the initiative and not only defeat the North Koreans at Inchon, but also retake Seoul two weeks later.[31] It is also extremely important to understand how critical maneuver is during spiritual warfare.

One of the most important ways to ensure that we do not lose our bitter spiritual war with the devil is to outmaneuver our enemy. As Sun

Tzu states, we should weigh the situation and then move, not the other way around. As with any other strategy or tactic, the only way we can outmaneuver the evil one is through the Holy Spirit's guidance on timing and maneuver. Movement can be in two directions...away from our vulnerabilities or towards the enemy's vulnerabilities. Through prayer, God's Word, time with our Lord, and wise counsel from brothers and sisters in Christ, He guides us to conduct ourselves in a way that will not allow the evil one to outmaneuver us.

**Plans fail for lack of counsel, but with many advisers they succeed.** (Proverbs 15:22, NIV)

**The plans of the righteous are just, but the advice of the wicked is deceitful.** (Proverbs 12:5, NIV)

Sun Tzu stated, "Those who do not follow local guides are unable to obtain the advantages of the ground." This is an excellent point. Whenever the U.S. Army deployed to a foreign theater of operation, it relied heavily on individuals from the local population to instruct it on the culture, location of the enemy, key terrain, water and food sources, and tenets of the language to name only a few. When I (John) was deployed to both Iraq and Afghanistan, we relied heavily on the population to provide us critical information on the local culture, key terrain, and locations and disposition of the enemy. We were able to prevent losses, develop effective strategies, and enlist local support.

Spiritually, we must rely on our one guide, our Lord Jesus, to help us outmaneuver the enemy. He will safely guide us out of imminent danger with the evil one and to places He has uniquely prepared for us to be. As the Creator and Sustainer of all life, He serves as the unwavering and perfect guide for all our lives. But the truth is that He uses His people, other brothers, and sisters to help us discern His ways. He uses times of verbal wrestling in small groups to open the Truths of His Word. Times of solitude and prayer bring understanding to His way for our lives. But we need to do the work of asking and being available to hear His guidance. This may be the most important point of not only this chapter but the entire book. Jesus is the *only* guide who can help us maneuver to a safe spiritual position and is the *only* complete protection we can have from the evil one's attacks. Take caution against following the wrong guide. There will be worldly teachings that sound good, right, or even biblical but are lies.

In this chapter of the Art of War, Sun Tzu stated the following: "And therefore those skilled in war avoid the enemy when his spirit is keen and attack him when it is sluggish, and his soldiers are homesick. This is control of the moral factor." Throughout history, most successful military battles are won by the general who achieves the element of surprise in an attack. Most experienced generals understand it is best to conduct an attack when the enemy is either sleeping or in the process of waking up and preparing for the day. The evil one understands this as well and will attack us when we are "sluggish" and not prepared for an attack.

**You are all children of the light and children of the day. We do not belong to the night or to the darkness. So then, let us not be like others, who are asleep, but let us be awake and sober.** (1 Thessalonians 5:5-6, NIV) Jesus understood this and told us in His Word to always be ready and to "stay awake." The evil one never rests; he is always on the hunt for an opportunity to attack us when we are "sluggish" and easily susceptible to sin. Real world examples include sexual immorality, substance abuse, gambling whether it be large or small amounts, and anything else that separates us from God's Commands. There are many more examples far less obvious that may not even look like sin on the surface. I'm spiritually sluggish when:

- I'm exceptionally busy.
- I compare myself and my work to others who appear to be surpassing my 'success'.
- I'm more concerned with what I don't have than grateful for what I do.
- I look at my emotions as facts instead of indicators.
- The people I hang out with or the content I consume visually or audibly are unhealthy.

We avoid being "sluggish" by conducting ourselves in a manner that glorifies God, and when we stumble, we repent and receive forgiveness from Jesus. On the other side of maneuver, God calls us to go when and where He needs us to do His kingdom work. So many times, this doesn't make sense from a human understanding, but God sees the big picture.

> **For my thoughts are not your thoughts, neither are your ways my ways, declares the Lord.** (Isaiah 55:8, ESV)

> **Many are the plans in the mind of a man, but it is the purpose of the Lord that will stand.** (Proverbs 19:21, ESV)

> **For we are his workmanship, created in Christ Jesus for good works, which God prepared beforehand, that we should walk in them.** (Ephesians 2:10, ESV)

A recent discussion with a fellow pastor highlighted how God uniquely chooses, equips, and uses people for His purposes. This new, young pastor encountered an individual who was possessed and needed an exorcism. This pastor was not trained in this area and felt ill equipped to handle the situation. Through prayer, the help of an additional pastor who had experience in this area, and by faithfully following God's lead, the man was freed from Satan's bondage. God has used this situation to open other Jesus followers' eyes to the truths of the spiritual warfare going on around us.

The Apostle Paul provides numerous accounts of the principle of maneuvering. We see times where God specifically leads him to ministry and times God prevents the movement Paul had determined.

> **While they were worshiping the Lord and fasting, the Holy Spirit said, "Set apart for me Barnabas and Saul for the work to which I have called them." Then after fasting and praying they laid their hands on them and sent them off.** (Acts 13:2-3, ESV)

> **And they went through the region of Phrygia and Galatia, having been forbidden by the Holy Spirit to speak the word in Asia. And when they had come up to Mysia, they attempted to go into Bithynia, but the Spirit of Jesus did not allow them. So, passing by Mysia, they went down to Troas. And a vision appeared to Paul in the night: a man of Macedonia was standing there, urging him and saying, "Come over to Macedonia and help us." And when Paul had seen the vision, immediately we sought to go on into Macedonia, concluding that God had called us to preach the gospel to them.** (Acts 16:6-10, ESV)

Consider the following quote from Sun Tzu: "Therefore, the art of employing troops is that when the enemy occupies high ground, do not confront him; with his back resting toward the hills, do not oppose him." Our goal in life through the Lord Jesus as our guide is to move toward the moral high ground. The truth is this high ground is impossible to fully occupy since by nature we are all sinful. However, we should constantly strive to keep our "back resting toward the hills" through prayer, Scripture study, and communion with Jesus. In His strength and guidance, we not only outmaneuver the evil one but also establish a position where we are secure from his attacks.

### Biblical Truths
1. God's counsel through His Word is the only counsel for His people.
2. God's people cannot see the whole picture.
3. God has prepared good for us to do.

### Questions
1. Do you normally weigh a situation before moving or do you move and then weigh the situation after some experience? What has happened? What is the value in each?
2. Who in your life do you count on for wise counsel? How often do you have meaningful conversations with this person?
3. What areas of your life cause you to be "sluggish" in fighting the spiritual battle you're in? Are there triggers that cause you to fall into this? How can you avoid these triggers?

### Tactics
1. Make prayer, time in God's Word, and solitude a daily habit. Use the prayer guide found in the Appendix 2.
2. Identify, solidify, and nurture relationships with people who can help you discern God's will and ways.

CHAPTER 8

# THE NINE VARIABLES

*"There are some roads not to follow; some troops not to strike; some cities not to assault; and some ground that should not be contested."* (Sun Tzu)

It is so easy to get sucked into every skirmish, but God does not call us to do battle at every turn. There are areas that are not ours to occupy. Likewise, God calls us to study and consider all these things prior to going to battle.

**Or what king, going out to encounter another king in war, will not sit down first and deliberate whether he is able with ten thousand to meet him who comes against him with twenty thousand? And if not, while the other is yet a great way off, he sends a delegation and asks for terms of peace.** (Luke 14:31-32, ESV)

In Chapter 8 in *The Art of War*, Sun Tzu describes "Nine Variables" that a successful general must understand. To illustrate just how important Sun Tzu thought these "Nine Variables" were, here are two of his quotes. "A general thoroughly versed in the advantages of the nine variable factors knows how to employ his troops." He goes on further, "The General who does not understand the advantages of the nine variables will not be able to use the ground to his advantage even though familiar with it." As Christians it is helpful to draw a correlation between each of the "Nine Variables" and how we can leverage the meaning in our struggle with the evil one. It's important to understand though, that in this unseen war we're in, only God himself sees, knows, and can use the "Nine Variables." However, each of us has found ourselves reeling from misunderstanding these "Nine Variables."

It is important to recognize that this chapter in the *Art of War* may be one of the most difficult to understand but is extremely important. To help in this, the following are the "Nine Variables" he highlights, and we have assigned numbers for easier future reference:

1. "You should not encamp in low-lying ground."
2. "In communicating ground, unite with your allies."
3. "You should not linger in desolate ground."
4. "In enclosed ground, resourcefulness is required."
5. "In death ground, fight."
6. "There are some roads not to follow."
7. "There are some troops not to strike."
8. "There are some cities not to assault."
9. "There is some ground which should not be contested."

So how do these apply to our lives as Christians in our own spiritual warfare? Let's look at each one individually.

## "You should not encamp in low-lying ground."

In military terms this refers to not staying too long in the low ground. If an enemy can catch an army while it is either moving through or bivouacking in an area that is lower in elevation, then it can easily launch artillery and direct fire attacks from the higher ground achieving more momentum. Fending off a major attack in a lower elevation is much more difficult. In the spiritual context this refers to multiple mental and spiritual states. The most critical one is an unrepentant state of sin. Ultimately, sin leads to spiritual sickness, a burdening of the conscience, and the possibility of falling away from the faith. The evil one uses sin to take a believer's eyes off Jesus, convict them of their guilt, and then whisper lies about God's unwillingness to love such a horrible sinner. A second state is living a worldly lifestyle surrounded by unbelievers. In this state, the evil one would have you start believing that scriptural truths and God's ways are outdated, not relevant, and not important. Again, Satan uses guilt, shame, bitterness, and all the emotions to distract and destroy.

> **The night is nearly over; the day is almost here. So let us put aside the deeds of darkness and put on the armor of light. Let us behave decently, as in the daytime, not in carousing and drunkenness, not in sexual**

immorality and debauchery, not in dissension and jealousy. Rather, clothe yourselves with the Lord Jesus Christ, and do not think about how to gratify the desires of the flesh.** (Romans 13:12-14, NIV)

Unlike the evil one, God would have all saved, and the Holy Spirit leads us to repentance. The good news is that God has given us many amazing gifts including confession and forgiveness! Satan's lies are dispelled, you are forgiven, and a child of the Most High God! When we linger and find ourselves mired in low-lying ground, He gives us the strength to leave it behind.

**For the Son of Man came to seek and to save the lost.** (Luke 19:10, ESV)

## "In communicating ground, unite with your allies."

In military terms this refers to a geographical area with many roads leading in and out. It is critical to ensure an army coordinates with its allies to secure the roads that are adjacent to them, so the enemy does not use them to outmaneuver its forces. When a force finds itself alone and not able to secure an area, the chances of defeat are great. Enemies can come from a variety of directions and catch a standing force off guard but with allies looking out for each other, victory is most assured. During World War II in The Battle of Britain (July 1940 through October 1940), Germany, as part of the Axis Powers, relentlessly bombed the United Kingdom (U.K.) in preparation for a potential ground invasion. In its weakened state, Britain was susceptible to a ground invasion even though it defeated Germany in this mostly air battle. However, the U.S. entered the war after the attack on Pearl Harbor by the Japanese on December 7, 1941, and began staging its Soldiers in the U.K. to help the beleaguered Allied Powers in the war against the Axis powers. This reinforcing effort by the U.S. eliminated the threat of a German invasion into the U.K. and served as the starting point to turn the tide of the war in Europe against Germany and her allies.[32]

In the spiritual context this refers to regularly looking out for each other and even carrying each other when needed. An important step to gain friends as allies is to gather with and get to know brothers and sisters in Christ. This can be done in small group settings, one-on-one accountability, and through attending worship. By doing these things, you remain in fellowship with other Christians and can encourage and strengthen one another in faith in Christ while watching out for each other. United, you are strong!

> **Let us hold unswervingly to the hope we profess, for he who promised is faithful. And let us consider how we may spur one another on toward love and good deeds, not giving up meeting together, as some are in the habit of doing, but encouraging one another—and all the more as you see the Day approaching.** (Hebrews 10:23-25, NIV)

> **Two are better than one,**
>   **because they have a good return for their labor:**
> **If either of them falls down,**
>   **one can help the other up.**
> **But pity anyone who falls**
>   **and has no one to help them up.**
> **Also, if two lie down together, they will keep warm.**
>   **But how can one keep warm alone?**
> **Though one may be overpowered,**
>   **two can defend themselves.**
> **A cord of three strands is not quickly broken.** (Ecclesiastes 4:9-12, NIV)

## "You should not linger in desolate ground."

In military terms this refers to an army not remaining in an area without resources such as food, shelter, and water. In a spiritual context, this refers to a person who lives in the darkness of their sinfulness and fails to engage in prayer, receive Holy Communion, or be in constant fellowship with other Christians.

> **If we claim to have fellowship with him and yet walk in the darkness, we lie and do not live out the truth. (1 John 1:6, NIV)**

Desolate ground is darkness, and it is dangerous to stay here.

## "In enclosed ground, resourcefulness is required."

Militarily, this refers to an army moving through mountains or forests. When terrain limits visibility, the army must be cautious and remain vigilant for surprise attacks from an enemy force or the hazards of nature. Spiritually, this refers to when an individual feels isolated and alone, not able to "see the forest for the trees." But God's Word assures us that we are not alone, and that God leads us and protects us even through this valley of the shadow of death. There's great power and comfort found only in Jesus who lifts His followers out of this feeling of despair. "Resourcefulness" is using the gifts of God in creative ways. For example, practice forgiving others and loving and praying for "enemies" as ways to handle attacks in enclosed ground.

**Even though I walk**
**through the valley of the shadow of death,**
**I will fear no evil,**
**for you are with me;**
**your rod and your staff,**
**they comfort me.** (Psalm 23:4, ESV)

## "In death ground, fight."

Death ground happens when an army is surrounded or finds itself in a very difficult, if not impossible, military position; it must fight to the death. In one respect, our whole life as Jesus followers is being fought on "death ground." The difference is that Christ followers have been given new life in Christ and are no longer dead in their sins. Christ won the "death ground" for us on the cross and empty tomb. But the battle for people's souls... a battle of death and life continues to rage on with many in peril. We sometimes feel this in our very souls when we realize that we are under perilous attack and must also fight to our physical death. Christians also find themselves battling for loved ones in this ground–children, family, and spouses who have rejected the faith. The only way to effectively fight these types of attacks is through the faith and strength given by the Holy Spirit. In faith, we die to self and take up our crosses as we stand. Through strong and constant prayer with our Lord and Savior Jesus and nourishment from God's Word, we stand. We should also seek help from our local pastors and elders of the church.

**Fight the good fight of the faith. Take hold of the eternal life to which you were called when you made your good confession in the presence of many witnesses.** (1 Timothy 6:12, NIV)

### "There are some roads not to follow."

Militarily, it would be disastrous to use roads that led into possible ambush situations or were incapable of handling the troop movement. The wrong road can lead to thinning of the troop movement, increasing vulnerability. It can also lead to bottlenecks in troop replenishments and set the stage for a potential disaster.

> **For the time will come when people will not put up with sound doctrine. Instead, to suit their own desires, they will gather around them a great number of teachers to say what their itching ears want to hear.** (2 Timothy 4:3, NIV)

> **For the Lord watches over the way of the righteous,**
> **but the way of the wicked leads to destruction.** (Psalm 1:6, NIV)

Rejection of sound doctrine carries a great risk. It takes you down a road that puts you in peril. Our forefathers battled this at every turn. The Creeds (Nicene, Apostles, and Athanasian) were written to combat false teachings which still exist today. There is a great risk in rejection of sound doctrine and in surrounding yourself with people who use cultural truths to make scripture more palatable. It's important to only use scripture to interpret scripture.

### "There are some troops not to strike."

Regardless of how strong a military force is, there are times when enemy forces and strength are greater. This happens when they have amassed adequate munitions, resources, and troops that would make it impossible to overcome. They also know the ground better. In martial arts training, you are taught that you will always find someone faster, stronger, and more proficient in the arts. When you do, the best course is to retreat and not engage. Even though we know Jesus has conquered the evil one and has ultimate power overall, caution must be exercised when confronting "troops" amassed by the evil one. Leaders, teachers and practitioners of Voodoo, Animism, New Age religions, wicca, and any of the other anti-Christian practices are troops to avoid. A Jesus follower must be uniquely called and prepared by God to engage certain troops.

> **Some Jews who went around driving out evil spirits tried to invoke the name of the Lord Jesus over those who were demon-possessed.**

They would say, "In the name of the Jesus whom Paul preaches, I command you to come out." Seven sons of Sceva, a Jewish chief priest, were doing this. One day the evil spirit answered them, "Jesus I know, and Paul I know about, but who are you?" Then the man who had the evil spirit jumped on them and overpowered them all. He gave them such a beating that they ran out of the house naked and bleeding. (Acts 19:13-17, NIV)

## "There are some cities not to assault."

During combat operations, an attacking force may bypass urban areas that are not necessary to accomplish their more important tactical and strategic objectives. U.S. Army doctrine considers this an important factor for military leaders during the planning and execution of an offensive campaign.[33] When a strategist considers troop deployment, it becomes clear that certain cities and areas are not worth the effort or cost of an assault. The potential loss of life and resource drain do not justify the tactical and strategic advantages gained by engaging. It also diverts resources away from more valuable targets. An example from 2022 is the Russian attempt to take Mariupol, Ukraine. After two months of strong resistance, considerable loss of life and resources, the Russians abandoned the siege but at great cost. It stands to reason they determined this was one of those cities not to be assaulted. When considering this variable from a spiritual perspective, we must continue to remind ourselves that God alone knows what lies ahead in any given "city." That city may be too fortified, it may not be the right timing, and/or the place for battle has not been prepared. Jesus warned his disciples about times they wouldn't be accepted and instructed them to leave those "cities."

**If anyone will not welcome you or listen to your words, leave that home or town and shake the dust off your feet.** (Matthew 10:14, NIV)

## "There is some ground that should not be contested."

A general must understand that it is not always prudent to attempt to gain ground in places where the enemy has a clear and insurmountable advantage. During World War II, the United States realized that a direct ground attack on the island of Japan would result in the loss of an incredible number of Soldiers. President Truman made the difficult decision to deploy atomic weapons to bring Japan, the enemy of the United States at the time, to heel. In the spiritual context this brings us back to the opening of this chapter. God does not want us to engage in battle at every turn but wants us to follow His will. In many cases, He calls on us instead to pray for our human enemies, to turn the other cheek, and to avoid confrontation. In our war with the evil one, we must exclusively rely on Jesus to guide and protect us. He gives us the spiritual armor we need. It's only in God's strength and through the Holy Spirit we can stand against the constant barrage of assaults.

As you can see, studying these "Nine Variables" instructs our daily battle against the evil one, but it is not easily grasped in one reading. All these "Variables" remind us that we must solely rely on Jesus and allow Him to sustain us through the gifts and means He has given us. When we enjoy constant communion with Him through prayer, grow in understanding of God's mercy and grace through Bible study, receive His true presence through Holy Communion, and draw strength and support from our fellow believers we are certain to recognize and know the Nine Variables. In turn, the battles we engage in will be those the Holy Spirit leads us to, and in that we can be certain of the outcome.

**Biblical Truths**
1. God will guide and lead us into the battles he would have you fight.
2. He wants us to follow Him as He guides us through the struggles with the evil one.
3. Jesus came to seek and save the lost and would have all people come to Him.

**Questions**
1. Which of the Nine Variables have you particularly ignored in terms of your spiritual well-being? What happened?
2. How do you know the path that God is leading you? What spiritual disciplines are critical to discerning that path?
3. What "ground" do you think you are in right now? What is your best next course of action?

**Tactics**
1. Study the Nine Variables as applied to Spiritual Warfare and become a student of assessing these in your life.
2. Identify areas of darkness and sin in your life. With God's help, take one step towards eliminating it.
3. Study, memorize, and recite the Apostles' Creed frequently.

## CHAPTER 9
# MARCHES

*An army prefers high ground to low, esteems sunlight and dislikes shade. Thus, while nourishing its health, the army occupies a firm position."*
(Sun Tzu)

Sun Tzu said, "Generally when taking up a position and confronting the enemy, having crossed the mountains, stay close to the valleys. Encamp on high ground facing the sunny side." When an army is engaging in combat operations, one of the cardinal tactical rules is that it must always strive to occupy the high ground. This holds true whether an army is fighting in the mountains, on the plains, in the jungle, or within a city or built-up area. This affords the army a significant tactical advantage against a determined enemy. One of the first lessons a young military leader learns while being schooled in military tactics and doctrine is this important principle.

Specifically, possessing the high ground allows one's forces to have longer fields of view of approaching enemy fighters coupled with the ability to shoot its direct fire using what in the military jargon is called plunging fire. Additionally, it is more advantageous for a military force to drop artillery on its approaching foe using mortars or other shorter range artillery cannons and munitions. Finally, it is much easier to defend the high ground against an attacking foe since its opponent must fight uphill. Fighting uphill against a well dug in adversary is physically exhausting and has historically proven very difficult to win. Sun Tzu reinforces this when he states, "Fight downhill; do not ascend to attack." At the Battle of Bunker Hill (June 17, 1775) during the American Revolutionary War,

1,200 Colonial troops occupied Bunker Hill to prevent the British from seizing the high ground and gaining control of Boston Harbor. Bunker Hill is in the heights outside of the City of Boston, Massachusetts, specifically in Charlestown, Massachusetts. Because of the Colonial position on Bunker Hill, it took the numerically superior British Soldiers (numbering over 3,000) three assaults on the hill to dislodge the colonists. The British incurred over 1,000 casualties in achieving this hard-fought victory. Although the British achieved victory, it cost them a significant amount of human resources and was a major factor in their ultimate decision to evacuate Boston. The Colonists effectively used high ground to achieve a strategic victory.[34]

Unfortunately, occupying high ground is one area that we, as humans, struggle with constantly. Our sinful nature prefers low ground and darkness. Our sinfulness would have us live in the shadows, the valleys, and in darkness.

**Everyone who does evil hates the light, and will not come into the light for fear that their deeds will be exposed.** (John 3:20, NIV)

It's an ongoing battle that is won or lost in our actions, our choice of friends, and in our strength to ward off the enemy's attacks. In the march of life's battle, it's so easy to get weary, lose heart, and not take care of ourselves. But God calls us to rest, to sabbath, to nourish our spiritual health. To occupy high ground in the light. But we are tempted each day by the pleasures and rewards of this world, all things that take us away from our God and leave us vulnerable. The evil one would have us live in darkness and despair, leaving us vulnerable to attacks.

However, we have been brought into the light by the Holy Spirit, and when we feed ourselves with God's Word, regular worship, time with God, and then surround ourselves with like-minded brothers and sisters, we bask in the sunlight and occupy the firm position.

**But you are a chosen people, a royal priesthood, a holy nation, God's special possession, that you may declare the praises of him who called you out of darkness into his wonderful light.** (1 Peter 2:9, NIV)

**For you were once darkness, but now you are light in the Lord. Live as children of light.** (Ephesians 5:8, NIV)

Living as children of light means preferring high ground, esteeming the light! So how do we do that as His people who are engaged, attacked, and harried by the enemy?

So how do we, as God's people, occupy high ground? Let's define "high ground" first. High ground is the place where God would have you be regarding your faith and trust, your lifestyle and friends, and your thinking and mental health. A good first step is to recognize that we cannot do this on our own. Left to our sinfulness, we would run to the shadows. However, the Holy Spirit has been given to strengthen, encourage and help us grow to be people who love light over darkness. As we grow in faith, we have a different worldview and aren't as tempted by the pleasures of this world. God has given His people gifts for learning, strengthening, and experiencing the high ground. God's Word teaches us about God, about His way of life, and encourages us. Baptism washes us clean in God's eyes. Through Baptism we are forgiven, given a new life, and receive the Holy Spirit. Through this gift, God gives us faith to believe in Jesus. God is with and in us through the Lord's Supper. It strengthens and nourishes as we receive forgiveness through the real presence of His body and blood in this meal.

As disciples of Jesus, we prefer the light of our Lord and despise the darkness of sin and evil. As we occupy high ground, we learn to love being in God's Word. We value time with God through prayer and solitude. Fed and nourished through His Word and the Lord's Supper, we find ourselves stronger, mentally, and spiritually healthy so that when the attacks come, we aren't exhausted and worn out. We fight downhill and return to the high ground to rest and prepare for the next foray.

During the infamous Battle of Little Big Horn, we can see a clear example of how seizing the high ground may have very well saved the U.S. forces from complete destruction. On June 25-26, 1876, near the Little Big Horn River in what was then the Montana Territory, the U.S. Cavalry Soldiers under the command of Lieutenant Colonel George Armstrong Custer fought against 3,000 Lakota Native Americans. This battle is correctly referred to as "Custer's Last Stand" because it indeed was his last stand. He, along with approximately 200 of his men, were killed by the Native Americans as they were eventually surrounded and overrun. However, during the battle several hundred of roughly 600 original Soldiers retreated to the bluffs (high ground) on the battlefield in various stages and were able to successfully hold off the continuously assaulting Native Americans for almost 24 hours until the Lakotas broke off the attack and left the area. Although the U.S. Army officers, including Custer, made many well documented tactical blunders during the battle, two leaders in charge of the remnant force were able to gain this contested high ground and use all its tactical advantages to ultimately save their lives.[35]

Sun Tzu stated, "In level ground occupy a position which facilitates your action. With heights to your rear and right, the field of battle is to the front and rear is safe." In the spiritual context, we must strive to occupy the level ground of faith. We live in the world but are not of the world. Through the power of the Holy Spirit, we can resist the temptations of sin that the evil one will constantly try to entice us into through our everyday lives.

**Rejoice always, pray continually, give thanks in all circumstances; for this is God's will for you in Christ Jesus.** (1 Thessalonians 5:16-18, NIV) The enemy understands that if he can lure us into sin, he will have a greater chance of separating us from our Lord Jesus. If he can successfully and permanently separate us from God, then the evil one has won the war against his victim. In other words, the evil one will try to remove us from the level ground of faith that is surrounded by the high ground of God's Truth. If he succeeds, we no longer have the spiritual advantage. It's critical that we do everything we can to avoid the low areas. We say no to situations and events that are against God's plan and will.

**Dear friends, I urge you, as foreigners and exiles, to abstain from sinful desires, which wage war against your soul. Live such good lives among the pagans that, though they accuse you of doing wrong, they may see your good deeds and glorify God on the day he visits us.**
(1 Peter 2:11-12, NIV)

Let's get real on what this looks like. And this won't be easy for some of you to read. Say no to that bachelor/bachelorette party. Don't go to the bar with a friend or meet with a person of the opposite sex without someone else being present. If you use curse words, do everything you can to break the habit. If you're tempted by pornography, don't allow yourself time alone to browse, install filters, and cancel any streaming services that give easy access. If the love of money is your weakness, give at least 10% away and increase your generosity 5% each year. If you crave power and prestige and find it's being fed at work, look for a different job and never take credit for the wins. Replace these with time with God, His Word, His gifts, and His people. Establish accountability partners, battle buddies, and retreat strategies. The Advisory Staff covered in Chapter 3 can help immensely in this area. Does this sound extreme? It is! We're in a war. We're talking about the difference between eternal life and eternal death.

**Flee the evil desires of youth and pursue righteousness, faith, love and peace, along with those who call on the Lord out of a pure heart.** (2 Timothy 2:22, NIV)

**Do not be yoked together with unbelievers. For what do righteousness and wickedness have in common? Or what fellowship can light have with darkness? What harmony is there between Christ and Belial? Or what does a believer have in common with an unbeliever?** (2 Corinthians 6:14-15, NIV)

It's interesting that scripture tells us that there is no temptation that we will have that can't be resisted with God's help. In fact, it says we are always given an out. So, take the out!

**No temptation has overtaken you except what is common to mankind. And God is faithful; he will not let you be tempted beyond what you can bear. But when you are tempted, he will also provide a way out so that you can endure it.** (1 Corinthians 10:13, NIV)

However, when we fall into sin and give up the high ground, which we are all susceptible to doing, we must run back to our Lord Jesus in repentance. Confession is so powerful whether done in the silence of our prayers, corporate confession in worship, or private confession to a friend or pastor. Hearing and believing the truth that you are forgiven is critical to regaining the high ground.

**If we confess our sins, he is faithful and just and will forgive us our sins and purify us from all unrighteousness.** (1 John 1:9, NIV)

Our God is faithful. He forgives and restores. It doesn't say that only certain sins are forgivable. It says He forgives, and He purifies! When we receive the amazing gift of forgiveness, we once again regain the tactical advantage over the evil one. We have in fact regained the moral high ground!

Sun Tzu stated, "An army prefers high ground to low, esteems sunlight and dislikes shade. Thus, while nourishing its health, the army occupies a firm position. An army that does not suffer from countless diseases is said to be certain of victory." Throughout the course of military campaigns, an army will continuously fight not only its human enemy but also disease and sickness not related to direct enemy contact. An Army that maintains good sanitation, eats healthy meats and vegetables, and has proper medicine on hand will have a marked advantage over an enemy that is inferior in this regard.

So high ground is important in the battle, but health is equally important. As holistic people, physical health affects our mental and spiritual health. Exercise, good sleep, and a healthy diet help Jesus followers resist sin. In the spiritual context, our souls need to be exercised and be regularly fed to help resist the evil one's attacks. We must continually pray and depend on our Lord Jesus to help us fight the temptation of sin. Sin is a disease! It is a disease and sickness that infects the human spirit and soul. Just like physical sickness, sin will drain an individual's energy and will to survive and it's contagious. The evil one clearly understands this and will seek to infect our spirits and souls with the disease of sin to weaken our resolve to maintain our critical relationship with our Lord Jesus. However, if a person feeds their soul on God's good gifts, they will stay spiritually strong. Through prayer, studying Holy Scripture, attending church regularly, and receiving the gift of the Lord's Supper, one can remain spiritually healthy and strong while they occupy high ground!

**Rejoice always, pray continually, give thanks in all circumstances; for this is God's will for you in Christ Jesus.** (1 Thessalonians 5:16-18, NIV)

### Biblical Truths
1. God always gives us an out from temptation.
2. He has given us His Word, the Lord's Supper, community, worship, prayer, and many disciplines to help us maintain the high ground.
3. Repentance and forgiveness are gifts given to help us regain the high ground when we fail.

**Questions**
1. Is money, sex, or power your biggest temptation? What examples do you have to support your answer?
2. Who are your battle buddies? How have you supported and helped each other stay on high ground?
3. What areas of your life–mental, physical, or spiritual– make you desire the low ground vs. the high ground? What can you do to mitigate this?

**Tactics**
1. Consistently attend worship to receive the gifts given through God's Word proclaimed, confession and forgiveness, and receiving the Lord's Supper. Take notes during worship identifying law and Gospel. Capture questions and new insights to reflect on during the week.
4. Develop and use retreat routes, battle buddies, and your Advisory Staff to help you stay on high ground.
5. Exercise, eat well, and get good rest. Take care of yourself physically.

## CHAPTER 10
# TERRAIN

*"And therefore I say: 'Know the enemy, know yourself' your victory will never be endangered. Know the ground, know the weather; your victory will then be total."* (Sun Tzu)

It's important that people engaged in battle know the "ground and weather." As Jesus followers, it is important that we become students of our culture and its trends. Not only should the Christian be a student of the culture, but it is also important to understand the prevalent Christian trends. Discernment will help us better prepare for waging the war.

"Take your Bible and take your newspaper and read both. But interpret newspapers from your Bible." (Karl Barth)

Sun Tzu stated that, "Ground may be classified according to its nature as accessible, entrapping, indecisive, constricted, precipitous, and distant." Military generals since the dawn of warfare understand that effective use of terrain is one of the most important factors for victory over their enemy. Countless books have been written about the impact of not only terrain, but more specifically how to best use terrain to gain a decisive advantage over one's enemy.

## Accessible Ground

Sun Tzu further stated, "Ground which both we and the enemy can traverse with equal ease is called accessible. In such ground, he who first takes the high sunny positions convenient to his supply routes can fight advantageously." In the military context, the principle of taking the high ground was discussed in detail in the last chapter. To put a finer point on this, it is important that an army must also ensure the ground it occupies can be re-supplied with food, water, medical supplies, and ammunition. If a general leads their forces onto the high ground, they risk the chance of the enemy cutting off all supply routes. Even though it may have the high ground, this puts the army in grave danger of being strangled due to a lack of critical supplies.

A similar thing can happen to a person spiritually. If an individual believes they are on the moral high ground but allows themselves to become complacent with their position, the evil one will surely look for an opportunity to surround and isolate the person from other Christians and ultimately Jesus. To prevent this from occurring, a person should and must look for opportunities to be in fellowship with other believers and remain in communion with the Lord Jesus. This was a critical part of the first church in Acts.

**And they devoted themselves to the apostles' teaching and the fellowship, to the breaking of bread and the prayers.** (Acts 2:42, ESV)

They understood the power and strength gained by meeting together and being in real fellowship with like-minded believers.

In scripture, Jesus followers are frequently referred to as sheep. Sheep are much safer in the flock with a shepherd watching over them. What a beautiful picture of the Church, sheep together enjoying God's gifts with God himself watching over and protecting us. Scripture warns His sheep of the perils.

**Go your way; behold, I am sending you out as lambs in the midst of wolves.** (Luke 10:3, ESV)

Scripture also teaches that, as we gather, God is present. It also teaches that He is truly present in the Lord's Supper through the bread and the wine. How powerful it is to be in God's presence! So, the key to terrain in this sense is not to let the evil one separate you from the flock or the Shepherd.

## Entrapping Ground

Sun Tzu continues, "Ground easy to get out of but difficult to return to is entrapping. The nature of this ground is such that if the enemy is unprepared and you sally out you may defeat him. If the enemy is prepared and you go out and engage, but do not win, it is difficult to return. This is unprofitable." Militarily, this means a general must be reasonably confident of victory before they leave favorable terrain for one that is less advantageous. For example, if an army marches down from the high ground to fight an enemy at a significantly lower elevation, and the enemy defeats the forces, it will be very difficult for the retreating army to climb back up and retain that piece of high ground.

## Indecisive Ground

"Ground equally disadvantageous for both the enemy and ourselves to enter is indecisive. The nature of this ground is such that although the enemy holds out a bait I do not go forth but entice him by marching off. When I have drawn out half his force, I can strike him advantageously." An example of this type of terrain is a densely wooded area. If both armies march into this type of terrain to fight, then neither will have much of a tactical advantage given that all the trees will reduce the range of their small arms weapons. It also makes artillery ineffective. Sun Tzu is correctly stating that rather than risk defeat, it is better to not engage the enemy and risk losing the complete military advantage. This leads into Sun Tzu's next statement in this chapter.

## Constricted Ground

"If I first occupy constricted ground I must block the passes and await the enemy. If the enemy first occupies such ground and blocks the defiles I should not follow him; if he does not block them completely I may do so." In this scenario, Sun Tzu refers to a piece of terrain that is likely a narrow pass or gorge between mountains or hills. In military terms, this is a route an army can only march through in what is called a narrow column or narrow front formation. Picture an army marching single file. When an army moves in this type of formation and comes under attack, it is very difficult for it to deploy into an attack formation or defend since it cannot mass combat power very easily. The best option for an army in this situation is to move quickly through the defile and once through it, either keep moving or block the defile and wait for the approaching enemy and then attack it as it attempts to move through the narrow and constricting terrain. This can be best illustrated with the following historical example that took place well over 2,000 years ago.

The Battle of Thermopylae (480 BCE) took place during the second invasion by Persia (modern day Iran) into what is Greece today. Sparta led an alliance of Greek City-states against the Persian Empire under the command of King Xerxes. Over the course of three days, the Greeks held back the advancing Persians by blocking their advance through a 4-mile-long narrow pass at a remote place at the time called Thermopylae. In the end the Greeks fell, and the Persians continued their march into Greece. The bravery of the Greeks, especially by the 300 Spartans serving as a rear-guard under the leadership of King Leonidas, caused Persia to lose an estimated 20,000 casualties. Whereas the Greeks only lost an estimated 2,000 men.[36] Sun Tzu goes on to state the following important tactical principle.

## Precipitous Ground

"In precipitous ground I must take position on the sunny heights and await the enemy. If at first he occupies such ground I lure him by marching off; I do not follow him." This goes back to what was discussed in the last chapter regarding the importance of seizing the high ground and holding it against an enemy attack. Sun Tzu correctly states that if the enemy seizes the high ground first, it is best to march away from it and not attack since doing so will not be easy and will result in a high number of casualties. When a force does engage a well-fortified enemy on the high ground, it must ensure it has overwhelming and superior combat power and is prepared to incur many casualties.

## Distant Ground

Sun Tzu next says, "When at a distance from an enemy of equal strength it is difficult to provoke battle and unprofitable to engage him in his chosen position." The U.S. Army follows a general rule; only attack a defender if you have a favorable force ratio advantage in combat power.[37] History has repeatedly shown that if an attacking formation does not have this type of advantage in numbers against a determined enemy, then it is very difficult to achieve victory. Oftentimes, the attacker will at best fight to a draw, but would lose the overall battle or be so weakened that the general cannot continue the long-term campaign until they replenish their force. Let's use an extreme example to put this in a spiritual context.

Should a Jesus follower join a wiccan coven so they could be used by God to bring the good news to them? Probably not, but we also know that our God is all-powerful and could use someone to do this. If you believe God has called you to engage the battle in this "terrain," only engage after significant wise Christian counsel, prayer, and discernment. And only after putting on the whole armor of God!

Finally, Sun Tzu summarizes his description of these principles with the following, "These are the principles relating to six different types of ground. It is the highest responsibility of the general to inquire into them with the utmost care." Sun Tzu is referring to what is called generalship in the military. That is the ability of the general to expertly analyze how all aspects of terrain will impact ongoing or impending military operations, specifically combat with the enemy. Failure to do so effectively could mean and often has meant defeat. However, there are countless examples throughout history where the general correctly understood how to use terrain effectively to defeat a determined enemy. An excellent military example is the Battle of Teutoburg Forest in 9 CE. The Battle of the Teutoburg Forest was one of the Roman Empire's worst defeats.

During this battle, the Germanic tribes, located in present day Germany, used the dense forests in the area to their tactical advantage. The Germanic forces were under the command of Arminius, a Germanic prince, who earned a strong reputation for his previous fighting on behalf of Rome. However, Arminius would later use the trust he gained with the Roman governor of Germania, Publius Quinctilius Varus, to betray Rome. Three Roman Legions numbering approximately 15,000 men under the command of Varus marched to suppress an alleged rebellion in the northwestern parts of Germania. Along their march, a Germania force of about 20,000 soldiers attacked the long-drawn-out column of Roman Soldiers in the thick vegetation. Due to the restricted terrain, the Roman legions could not effectively maneuver against the attacking force. Through a series of hit and run tactics over several days, all three Roman legions were destroyed. Once Varus learned of this disaster, he committed suicide in disgrace.[38]

We must use "terrain" to our advantage and not to our peril. So, let's get practical. Let's define "terrain" in spiritual terms as the "culture" or the places we live or hang out. Now, using other extreme examples, let's put "terrain" into the spiritual battle context. If a person is always hanging out at the bar, strip clubs, and places where the evil one is having a heyday, they are occupying dangerous ground. This is compounded if most friends are not Jesus followers with a biblical worldview. Again, dangerous ground. Ostensibly no way out, no supply in, surrounded by the enemy. Not a good place to be with the evil one on the prowl.

    During a business trip my peers decided to go to a strip club after dinner. I told them I (Gerry) didn't want to, so they agreed to drop me off before they went. On the way back from dinner to my dismay, they pulled into the strip club at least five miles away from the hotel. I found myself on dangerous ground. Instead of going in with them, God gave me the strength to go to a pay phone on the street, call a cab, and leave without entering even more dangerous territory. I had an out and took it. Unfortunately, if we don't think ahead, we can find ourselves in terrain that gives us no out. It's critical to think through situations prior to encountering them and develop plans to protect. God always gives us a way out.

    **No temptation has overtaken you except what is common to mankind. And God is faithful; he will not let you be tempted beyond what you can bear. But when you are tempted, he will also provide a way out so that you can endure it.** (1 Corinthians 10:13, NIV)

Another example we've heard too many times is from people who succumb to the temptation to commit adultery. You've heard it, maybe even experienced it. People befriend others at work. They develop a great working relationship and start to trust and depend on each other. That leads to more familiarity and ultimately puts them in dangerous terrain. Many times, it starts with a trip together or an "innocent" social meeting. Friendship, familiarity, flirtation, and rationalization occurs. It then too often leads to mental or physical adultery with either one or the other fantasizing and taking the relationship further than it should. Scripture says to flee! Sun Tzu would say don't even attempt to pass through this ground.

    **But you, man of God, flee from all this, and pursue righteousness, godliness, faith, love, endurance and gentleness.** (1 Timothy 6:11, NIV)

Sun Tzu concludes the chapter with, "And therefore I say: 'Know the enemy, know yourself' your victory will never be endangered. Know the ground, know the weather; your victory will then be total." Military leaders still widely reference this quote today. The words are simple, but as critical as the tenets are, they have often proved difficult to follow by military leaders throughout the centuries. However, the generals who have implemented all the above, especially terrain, have also proven to be very successful.

In a spiritual war, these tenets are also critical. Jesus followers must be students of the culture and God's Word. As a student studies God's Word and uses it to interpret the "terrain", the Holy Spirit will continue to provide discernment, strength, and ability to stay the course even in the worst possible ground.

**Biblical Truths**
1. We are lambs amid wolves and some "terrain" is more dangerous to our faith than others.
2. God is faithful and always provides a way out of temptation.
3. The best action we can take is to flee sin.
4. Strength comes from being in community with Christians.

**Questions**
1. What type of terrain do you find yourself in most of the time? Which place is the most dangerous to your faith walk... work, family, church, entertainment, etc.? How could you reduce time spent in dangerous "terrain"?
2. What steps can you take to prevent getting into "entrapping" ground? How can you better see and take the "out" God gives when temptation strikes?
3. How do you interpret news and life through a biblical perspective? Give examples.

**Tactics**
1. Be in constant, consistent fellowship with other Christian brothers and sisters. Join or start a small group and participate in it frequently.

Read and listen to the news, podcasts, worldviews with a Bible in hand. Use it to interpret.
2. Ruthlessly eliminate times spent in dangerous "terrain" and develop other outlets.

CHAPTER 11

# NINE VARIETIES OF GROUND

*"In respect to employment of troops, ground may be classified as dispersive, frontier, key, communicating, focal, serious, difficult, encircled, and death."* (Sun Tzu)

In the previous chapter we discussed the importance of knowing the "terrain." Now we will consider varieties of terrain. The similarity of these two concepts can be confusing and could lead to merging them together. But, in warfare, it's important to differentiate the two. "Varieties in Ground" in Sun Tzu's writings are the other factors that the physicality of "terrain" does not consider. In some respects, "varieties" is the context of "terrain." For example, you could be occupying high ground "terrain" that is classified as "dispersive ground." Depending on the classification, the moves and response of an army changes. So, in addition to identifying the "terrain" you're in, it's important to determine what variety of ground you are in and to develop strategies and tactics for each. Sun Tzu identifies and discusses nine different varieties that an army could operate in during its campaign. In regular and spiritual warfare some are more favorable than others.

## Dispersive Ground

"When a feudal lord fights in his own territory, he is in dispersive ground." Sun Tzu is referring to an army fighting in its own homeland. In this type of ground, it becomes much more difficult to keep the soldiers focused because the proximity to family and friends may tempt them to prioritize the individual safety of their loved ones over the collective mission. Based on this Sun Tzu goes on further with this wisdom, "And therefore, do not fight in dispersive ground; do not stop in the frontier borderlands." However, if an army must fight in this situation, then Sun Tzu states, "In dispersive ground I would unify the determination of the army."

There is probably no greater unifying or motivating factor for an army to come together than with the sole purpose to defend its loved ones. Such a "determination" will drive an army to push itself to its utmost limits to protect its beloved homeland. We see this real-world example today with the war in the Ukraine, where the citizens of that country are fiercely fighting to protect its people and territory from the invasion of Russia.

In spiritual warfare, we can consider "dispersive" ground in a similar way. It is so easy to get distracted by family and friends when called into God's kingdom work. We want to care for, be with, and protect our loved ones. In more and more family systems, being a Jesus follower is not encouraged, supported, or accepted. But Jesus uses a parable to warn about this thinking and to emphasize the priorities a Jesus follower should consider.

**As they were walking along the road, a man said to him, "I will follow you wherever you go." Jesus replied, "Foxes have dens and birds have nests, but the Son of Man has no place to lay his head." He said to another man, "Follow me." But he replied, "Lord, first let me go and bury my father." Jesus said to him, "Let the dead bury their own dead, but you go and proclaim the kingdom of God." Still another said, "I will follow you, Lord; but first let me go back and say goodbye to my family." Jesus replied, "No one who puts a hand to the plow and looks back is fit for service in the kingdom of God."** (Luke 9:57-62, NIV)

Jesus emphasizes the importance of keeping our eyes on Him and on His mission. What a stark example we see when Jesus essentially rejects his own family.

**Then Jesus' mother and brothers arrived. Standing outside, they sent someone in to call him. A crowd was sitting around him, and they told him, "Your mother and brothers are outside looking for you." "Who are my mother and my brothers?" he asked. Then he looked at those seated in a circle around him and said, "Here are my mother and my brothers! Whoever does God's will is my brother and sister and mother."** (Mark 3:31-35, NIV)

The rewards are great in following Jesus' mission.

**Then Peter spoke up, "We have left everything to follow you!" "Truly I tell you," Jesus replied, "no one who has left home or brothers or sisters or mother or father or children or fields for me and the gospel will fail to receive a hundred times as much in this present age: homes, brothers, sisters, mothers, children and fields—along with persecutions—and in the age to come eternal life."** (Mark 10:28-30, NIV)

The unifying factor is God's grace and love for all. He would save all and He alone can save. As His warriors, people already experiencing His free gifts, we are united with Him and are called to bring the Good News of salvation and forgiveness to enemy territory. We must resist distraction while we're in dispersive ground.

## Frontier Ground

"When he makes but a shallow penetration into enemy territory, he is in frontier ground...In frontier ground I would keep my forces closely linked." (Sun Tzu) When an army is only in shallow enemy territory, it is very easy for its soldiers to lose heart and have a desire to back track out of the enemy territory and head back to their homes. Sun Tzu recommends keeping its forces "closely linked" to prevent whole scale desertions. In ancient warfare, mass desertions were a constant fear of a general. Desertion was considered the worst form of cowardice and treason and was usually punishable by public execution in front of the army. This was done to send a strong warning to the ranks that this type of action would not be tolerated.

As Jesus followers become more mission minded, this is the ground they will find themselves in at first. The first encounters with people aligned with the evil one can be very intense and often disheartening. When faced with well-prepared, angry atheists and agnostics, new missionaries in new territories run back to the church without any desire to encounter the opposition again! If they are closely linked with stronger, more experienced "missionaries", they are more likely to continue beyond frontier ground. Being serious students of God's Word also helps link all of God's people together. Thanks be to God that He forgives and continues to encourage His sons and daughters!

He who descended is the very one who ascended higher than all the heavens, in order to fill the whole universe. So Christ himself gave the apostles, the prophets, the evangelists, the pastors and teachers, to equip his people for works of service, so that the body of Christ may be built up until we all reach unity in the faith and in the knowledge of the Son of God and become mature, attaining to the whole measure of the fullness of Christ. Then we will no longer be infants, tossed back and forth by the waves, and blown here and there by every wind of teaching and by the cunning and craftiness of people in their deceitful scheming. (Ephesians 4:10-14, NIV)

## Key and Communicating Ground

"Ground equally advantageous for the enemy or me to occupy is key ground...In key ground I would hasten up my rear elements." (Sun Tzu) We have previously discussed this in detail. If an army has possession of the key "ground", then it must quickly solidify its gains and mount a defense to hold it against an almost certain enemy counterattack. Sun Tzu goes on to talk about the effects of "communicating ground."

"Ground equally accessible to both the enemy and me is communicating...In communicating ground I would pay strict attention to my defences." Sun Tzu encourages preparing one's defense against an enemy who has equal access to a piece of terrain as one's own forces. When an army is in this type of terrain, it must be extra vigilant to always maintain security against an enemy that will try to attack it while unprepared.

Sun Tzu closes this part of his writings with, "Do not attack an enemy who occupies key ground; in communicating ground do not allow your formations to become separated." Again, an army that attacks its enemy that occupies high ground will usually not have the advantage. Even if it does have the advantage, any attack against the high ground will result in a high number of casualties. In communicating ground, neither side has a clear advantage, so such an attack has only a fifty percent chance for success if one assumes the enemy will be equally as vigilant.

This type of ground can be found in many places within the Christian community. Small groups meeting for Bible study without mature faith leadership. Jesus followers serving in the community and being tempted by non-biblical worldviews. Interest groups meeting at brewpubs to make people comfortable and hopefully reach others. These are all possible examples. They may all be communicating or key ground, not in and of themselves bad but all requiring vigilance. If a church or individual finds themselves in key or communicating ground, it is best to take a defensive posture. This includes practicing the spiritual disciplines spoken of before–worship, prayer, fasting, solitude. It also includes being extra watchful for the evil one's moves.

**Be alert and of sober mind. Your enemy the devil prowls around like a roaring lion looking for someone to devour.** (1 Peter 5:8, NIV)

## Focal Ground

"When a state is enclosed by three other states its territory is focal. He who gets control of it will gain the support of All-Under-Heaven...In focal ground, ally with neighbouring states; in deep ground, plunder...In focal ground I would strengthen my alliances." Sun Tzu's recommendation to make alliances with the neighboring states is imperative for an invading army. If the other states that are bordering the attacking army decide to attack, then its forces will be at potentially serious risk of being defeated and even annihilated. It would be very difficult for an army to attack in three different directions and equally difficult to defend in three different directions. Thus, militarily these alliances are critical to the success of the attacking army. During World War II, Adolf Hitler, the sinister Chancellor of Germany, directed his military forces to invade Russia on June 22, 1941. There has been much written on the "Eastern Front" of World War II, but the important point to illustrate in the context of Sun Tzu's words is that Joseph Stalin, the dictator of Russia at the time, worked diligently to bring the countries of the United Kingdom and the United States into his fold. During all their interactions, Stalin pleaded with the U.S. and U.K. leaders–President Franklin Roosevelt and Prime Minister Winston Churchill–to open a Western front to force Germany to fight in two different directions and alleviate the pressure against his battered nation. In the end, the U.S. and U.K. did invade Germany through France, and this did indeed achieve what Stalin hoped would be enough to allow his forces to beat back the German invasion and be able to assume the offensive.[39]

There are many different "tribes" of Jesus followers including many denominations and non-denominations. The differences in doctrine and theology range from great to minor but the evil one does everything he can to keep us divided. Differences are used by the evil one to keep us from becoming allies with each other against our common enemy, Satan, and his evil demons. Many practicing Christians believe we are sinful, in need of a Savior, and Jesus is the only way for salvation. In many respects we occupy focal ground every day of our lives and desperately need alliances with other Jesus followers to resist the attacks.

**As Scripture says, "Anyone who believes in him will never be put to shame." For there is no difference between Jew and Gentile—the same Lord is Lord of all and richly blesses all who call on him, for, "Everyone who calls on the name of the Lord will be saved."** (Romans 10:11-13, NIV) But there's also a caution. Be careful who you align with because the evil one has infiltrated and uses division to put obstacles in the way. There are many churches calling themselves "Christian" that teach that there are many ways to heaven, not just Jesus. Beware! It would be better to face the evil one alone than to inadvertently align with him.

**I urge you, brothers and sisters, to watch out for those who cause divisions and put obstacles in your way that are contrary to the teaching you have learned. Keep away from them.** (Romans 16:17, NIV)

## Serious Ground

"When the army has penetrated deep into hostile territory, leaving far behind many enemy cities and towns, it is in serious ground...In serious ground I would ensure a continuous flow of provisions." This dictum refers to what the military calls its lines of communications. This is a fancy way of stating that the route in which an army's supplies flow must remain unimpeded to keep it stocked with ammunition, food, water, and medical supplies at a minimum. During World War II, Germany attacked deep into Russian territory. Germany's overextension of its supply lines was one of the major reasons the Russian army was able to stop their attack, counterattack, and ultimately defeat them. Toward the end of the campaign, Germany could no longer supply its forces.

This resulted in catastrophic casualties for Germany. This significant loss of resources largely contributed to Germany's ultimate defeat by the Allied Forces.

Missionaries are obvious examples of Jesus followers being in "serious" ground. If missionaries cut themselves off from mental and spiritual support, they become vulnerable and prone to losing any ground they have gained. If they become lax in their spiritual disciplines, they are in even more peril. Many develop prayer support teams, accountability partners, and mentors to support their efforts. This continual flow of support and care helps them make gains in serious ground.

## Difficult Ground

"When the Army traverses mountains, forests, precipitous country, or marches through defiles, marshlands, or swamps, or any place where the going is hard, it is in difficult ground...In difficult ground I would press on over the roads." The reason Sun Tzu recommends using the roads is because they allow greater mobility for the army to move toward its objective. If the army tries to traverse difficult terrain, it risks getting bogged down and significantly slowing its rate of march. This would provide opportunities for its enemy to mount ambush type attacks in the restrictive terrain and attrit the army. By using roads, there is some risk; however, the attacking army could rely on speed to help ensure the enemy does not have the time to mount effective attacks or ambushes.

When the ground is "difficult" ground, life and the evil one create havoc, it's easy to get bogged down. Pride and self-sufficiency sometimes kick in and many decide they will go it alone and pave their own "roads" so to speak. Others are so weary they just want to quit and sit alone in the muck hoping it will all go away. Both are dangerous. Many solid resources, "roads", are available to the Jesus followers. For example, God has given us community to help each other press on and follow God's path.

**Brothers and sisters, I do not consider myself yet to have taken hold of it. But one thing I do: Forgetting what is behind and straining toward what is ahead, I press on toward the goal to win the prize for which God has called me heavenward in Christ Jesus.** (Philippians 3:13-14, NIV)

## Encircled Ground

"Ground to which access is constricted, where the way out is tortuous, and where a small enemy force can strike my larger one is called 'encircled'...In encircled ground I would block the points of access and egress." (Sun Tzu) To stop the enemy from gaining an advantage the army must block the attack routes the enemy might use to conduct its attack.

You may be there now. Feeling surrounded by evil, temptations on every side, no obvious way out, and in pain. There are times that a Christian should just hunker down and protect all access. When you realize you're in encircled ground, surround yourself with trusted brothers and sisters in Christ. Study God's Word even more fervently, pray unceasingly, and listen for God's direction. Shut down anything that would take you away from God's path. Depend on the Holy Spirit's guidance and strength. **But the Lord is faithful, and he will strengthen you and protect you from the evil one.** (2 Thessalonians 3:3, NIV)

## Death Ground

"Ground in which the army survives only if it fights with the courage of desperation is called 'death'...For it is the nature of soldiers to resist when surrounded; to fight to the death when there is no alternative, and when desperate to follow commands implicitly...in death ground fight." (Sun Tzu) When Soldiers find themselves in this type of dire situation, the only alternative they have is to fight to the death—that is the death of either themselves or their enemy. It is critical in this scenario that the general make it painfully clear to the army that they must fight or die. There is no surrender, but rather only death. Either their death or the death of their foe.

A graphic example of this is the Battle of Landing Zone (LZ) X-Ray in the Ia Drang Valley, Republic of Vietnam during the U.S. conflict in Vietnam. 1st Battalion, 7th Cavalry Regiment was the primary unit with several other supporting units. The U.S. Commander was Lieutenant Colonel Hal Moore, and the battle took place November 14–16, 1965. After the battalion was air assaulted to LZ X-Ray, it was quickly surrounded and placed under heavy fire from a numerically superior North Vietnamese force. Yet, after three days of brutal close combat, the American forces were able to drive back the North Vietnamese forces, largely through the support of air power and heavy artillery bombardment, which the North Vietnamese lacked. The United States claimed LZ X-Ray as a tactical victory, citing a 10:1 kill ratio.[40]

Jesus followers understand we are in a battle that ends in death and in many ways, we are on death ground on this earth. The real question is where eternity will be spent. Those who have faith in Jesus will have eternal life with Him. Those who do not will be eternally separated from God and all the gifts He gives. So as His people, who have been brought into faith and eternal life in Him, we fight for people from all nations to experience eternal life with Jesus, not eternal damnation with the evil one. We fight with the hope and confidence that Jesus went to the cross, died to pay for our sins, and rose again in victory over sin, death, and the devil. Jesus conquered Satan, but the struggle for the life of souls is real and vicious.

**Because of the increase of wickedness, the love of most will grow cold, but the one who stands firm to the end will be saved. And this gospel of the kingdom will be preached in the whole world as a testimony to all nations, and then the end will come.** (Matthew 24:12-14, NIV)

Sun Tzu described the nine types of terrain that an army could experience during its campaign with recommendations for how to operate in each type. From a military perspective, some types of terrain are clearly more advantageous than others. One of the keys to victory for an army is for the general to choose the most favorable type of terrain to conduct its military operations or choose a combination of several and use the best tactics while operating in each type. This often requires a combination of art and experience. In the end, the side which does this most effectively will usually emerge the victor.

Similar truths exist for the Jesus follower. Identifying and understanding the nine types of terrain are important. Choosing the most favorable type of terrain and avoiding the worst help an individual's faith walk. Through experience and fellowship with other believers, appropriate tactics and actions can be determined for the best possible outcomes.

### Biblical Truths
1. Jesus has defeated sin, death, and the devil.
2. The Lord is faithful and will strengthen and protect you for the battle.
3. False teachings will abound, but God will give discernment through His Word.

### Questions
1. Which variety of ground do you find the most challenging? How could you be best prepared for each variety?
2. Did you agree with the author's assessment that we are in both "focal" and "death" ground here on earth? Why or why not?
3. Why is it important to understand the variety of ground you're in? How can you be a better student of the "ground"?

### Tactics
1. Daily remind yourself of and recommit yourself to God's mission to seek and save the lost.
2. Study the Bible (not just reading) and incorporate devotional time into your daily routine. Enlist a battle buddy for accountability.
3. Re-read this chapter and become an expert in discerning which variety of ground you are in.
4. Write out tactics you will use for each "ground" variety.

## CHAPTER 12
# ATTACK BY FIRE

*"There are five methods of attacking with fire. The first is to burn personnel; the second, to burn stores; the third, to burn equipment; the fourth to burn arsenals; and fifth, to use incendiary missiles."* (Sun Tzu)

Sometimes in battles we are called to set things on fire. What does that look like? We are sometimes called to take strong stands for God and His Truth regardless of the cost. This chapter will give the reader the opportunity to develop perimeters and force level responses in preparation for those times.

Sun Tzu's five attacks by fire in the quote above are the different offensive techniques an army over 2,000 years ago could employ fire to inflict damage on its enemy. Each one of these techniques could be effective during his period depending on the type of tactical situation an Army found itself in while conducting military operations. Today, modern armies employ different methods of "fire." However, it is important to understand that merely using "fire" is not enough to bring a determined enemy to heel. The employment of "fire" is one of several tools an army has in their tool kit to help them achieve victory. Therefore, it is important to understand how modern military forces use "fire" in their tactics today.

An air force uses different types of bombs; whereas an artillery unit uses various types of explosive or incendiary munitions to weaken its enemy. As technology has progressed, the sophistication and destructive power of munitions has significantly increased. Most modern armies understand that to gain victory it must successfully outmaneuver its enemy.

Outmaneuvering an enemy simply means placing your army in a position of advantage over your enemy. In simple tactical terms, maneuver consists of fire and movement.[41] An advancing unit will often use a synchronous combination of direct fires (machine guns, small arms) and indirect fires (air force bombs, ground artillery explosive munitions) to conduct a successful maneuver. To better understand this concept, consider the following illustration.

If an infantry company wishes to seize a piece of decisive terrain it might first use one of its platoons of 30-40 soldiers to establish a base of direct machine gun fire against the enemy. While this happens, the commander directs the air force and ground artillery units to bombard this piece of decisive terrain. The intent is to not only destroy the enemy soldiers but also prevent them from placing effective direct and indirect fire on the advancing unit. Simultaneously, the infantry company commander will tactically move one or two platoons to charge the piece of terrain and seize it. Of course, all of this requires precise synchronization to prevent the movement of one's advancing units into its own indirect fire. Moreover, most good military leaders understand that it is extremely difficult and risky to advance its forces against a determined enemy without using indirect fires. Again, effective maneuver requires a combination of fire and movement. A classic example is the battle for Iwo Jima during World War II.

The Battle of Iwo Jima took place in the Pacific Theater of Operation during World War II. The invasion of this Japanese held island would represent the largest deployment–approximately 70,000–of U.S. Marines in combat in the history of the United States. It was also one of the bloodiest battles during World War II. Iwo Jima is an island about five miles long and two and half miles at its widest point. Prior to the war and the Japanese invasion, only about 500 inhabitants resided on this volcanic island. The attack which began on February 19, 1945, was called Operation Detachment. The island held significant strategic importance to the U.S. because it allowed the Americans to possess three airfields from which to stage future attacks against the Japanese mainland.

During the initial planning, U.S. military leaders projected the battle would be over in a week. However, their projections were not only overly optimistic but also flat out wrong. The battle lasted 36 days, and the Americans had to fight and pay for every inch of the ground with their blood. Optimism on the part of the American military planners stemmed from their belief that through the massive bombardment ("fire") of the Japanese defenders, they could inflict severe casualties on them even before a single Marine set foot on the island. Unfortunately, their assumptions were wrong. "Fire" alone would not bring the Americans an easy victory.

The U.S. began the battle by dropping 6,800 tons of bombs and 22,000 naval shells on the island! Clearly this is an example of Sun Tzu's attack by fire in the more modern age of warfare. However, despite all the bombs the U.S. hurled at the 20,000 Japanese defenders, the U.S. Marines, numbering 70,000, progressed slowly and with significant difficulty since the Japanese were well dug in with much protective overhead cover. All the attacks by fire would not have been enough for the U.S. to achieve victory in this bloody battle; victory required deployment of the U.S. Marines.

The battle lasted 36 days, and finally on March 26, the U.S. declared the island secure. In the end, the Americans killed approximately 18,000 Japanese soldiers and captured several hundred prisoners. On the other hand, the U.S. suffered 7,000 killed in action with another 20,000 wounded. Based on the severe loss of life and the large number of wounded personnel on both sides in this battle,[42] Sun Tzu's next words of counsel seem relevant in all ages of warfare.

"If not in the interest of the state, do not act. If you cannot succeed, do not use troops. If you are not in danger, do not fight." Clearly, Sun Tzu cautions against using troops if it is not in the best interest of the state and there is no clear path to victory. He recognized the cost in a nation's human resources must be preserved and committed only when necessary.

Unfortunately, the Battle of Iwo Jima is only one of many examples throughout the history of warfare where an incredible number of human lives have been sacrificed to achieve strategic and/or short term operational and tactical gains. Several years after this historic battle, multiple military leaders and historians speculated on the necessity of taking Iwo Jima given the extraordinary number of U.S. casualties. To put a finer point on this counsel, Sun Tzu continues with the following statement. "A sovereign cannot raise an army because he is enraged, nor can a general fight because he is resentful. For while an angered man may again be happy, and a resentful man again be pleased, a state that has perished cannot be restored, nor can the dead be brought back to life... Therefore, the enlightened ruler is prudent, and the good general is warned against rash action. Thus, the state is kept secure, and the army preserved." An ongoing counterexample to these wise words is the War in the Ukraine.

Russia launched an invasion on its Southern neighbor, the Nation of Ukraine, on February 24, 2022. The reasons for the invasion and the events leading up to this are beyond the scope of this book; however, it should be noted that most of the World including the United States condemned Russia for this unprovoked attack and issued severe sanctions against the Russian government. The Russian government believed that shortly after their invasion, the Ukrainian government would quickly capitulate. However, as most individuals reading this book know, Russia struggled for a protracted time attempting to achieve its strategic goals, and the Ukrainians mounted an effective defense and even went on the counterattack against a much more powerful army. Although Russia didn't share its exact casualty count with the world, U.S. military experts believe Russian troops suffered very high casualties. As of the time of this book's writing, the war in the Ukraine is ongoing.

Sun Tzu shares the five ways an army can employ "fire" followed by counsel cautioning against hastily and ill-thought-out use of one's military forces to prevent the unnecessary loss of precious Human Resources. However, in most battles it is impossible to achieve victory with only the use of "fire" as we have seen in one prominent historical example. Yet, to Sun Tzu's points, if a nation determines it is critical to achieve its strategic objectives, then it must carefully plan the use of military force that incorporates all the tools including "fire" for its army to successfully maneuver–effective use of fire coupled with movement to place its enemy at a disadvantage. This requires deliberate planning, coordination, and synchronized execution to achieve victory at the least cost of human life for one's army.

So, what is the use of "fire" in the context of the spiritual battles we encounter? Looking at scripture, the offensive weapon we are given is the Word of God. Martin Luther had a lot to say about this.

Besides, it is an exceedingly effectual help against the devil, the world, the flesh, and all evil thought to be occupied with the Word of God, to speak of it, and meditate on it. Therefore Ps. 1:2 declares those blessed who meditate on the Law of God day and night. Without a doubt you cannot offer a more effective incense or other fumigation to vex the devil than busying yourself with God's commandments and words, speaking, singing, or thinking of them. For this is indeed the true holy water and sign before which the devil flees and by which a man may drive him away.

Now for this reason alone you should gladly read, speak, think, and treat of these things even if you had no other fruit and benefit from them than the ability to drive away the devil and evil thoughts. For he cannot hear or endure God's Word. Nor is the Word of God like an idle tale such as that about Dietrich of Berne; but, as St. Paul says (Rom. 1:16), it is "the power of God," yes, indeed, the power of God which causes the devil the deepest anguish but strengthens, comforts, and helps us beyond measure.

But why should I speak of this at length? If I were to recount every benefit and fruit which God's Word produces, whence would I get enough paper and time? The devil is called the master of a thousand tricks. But what shall we call God's Word, which drives away and brings to naught this master of a thousand tricks with all his skill and power? It must indeed be the master of more than a hundred thousand tricks. And shall we frivolously despise such power, benefit, strength, and fruit- especially we who profess to be pastors and preachers? If so, we should not only have nothing to eat, but we should be driven out, baited by dogs, and pelted with dung, not only because we need all this every day as we need our daily bread but also because we must use it against the daily and unabated attack and ambush of the devil, the master of a thousand tricks.[43]

The challenge we have as sinful human beings is that we too often forget the enemy is Satan, not fellow human sinners. When rejected or harassed by those not-yet Jesus followers, we often want God's wrath to rain down on them. Effectively following Sun Tzu's first use of fire. The disciples fell into this trap also.

**And he sent messengers on ahead, who went into a Samaritan village to get things ready for him; but the people there did not welcome him, because he was heading for Jerusalem. When the disciples James and**

John saw this, they asked, "Lord, do you want us to call fire down from heaven to destroy them?" But Jesus turned and rebuked them. (Luke 9:52-55, NIV)

When we use "fire" in this way, many are hurt and burned. But God's way is different. We are to pray for our enemies, love them as ourselves, and share God's Word so the Holy Spirit can convict them of their need for Jesus. We are to show them the amazing free gift of mercy, grace, and forgiveness that God provides in Jesus. It's interesting to note that doing this can result in "fire."

**To the contrary, "if your enemy is hungry, feed him; if he is thirsty, give him something to drink; for by so doing you will heap burning coals on his head.** (Romans 12:20, ESV)

To attack our true enemy, the devil, and demons, we've been given authority in Jesus' name to use a powerful weapon, God's Word. Jesus used it to cast out demons, shut their mouths, resist temptation, and make the enemy tremble in fear. It is efficacious, active, and alive.

**For the word of God is alive and active. Sharper than any double-edged sword, it penetrates even to dividing soul and spirit, joints and marrow; it judges the thoughts and attitudes of the heart.** (Hebrews 4:12, NIV)

This truth is also captured powerfully in verse three of the hymn, A Mighty Fortress.

> And though this world, with devils filled,
> should threaten to undo us,
> we will not fear, for God has willed
> his truth to triumph through us.
> The prince of darkness grim,
> we tremble not for him;
> his rage we can endure,
> for lo! his doom is sure;
> one little word shall fell him.
> Martin Luther, (1529); translator Frederick H. Hedge (1852) hymnary.org, Public Domain

As people chosen and redeemed by God, we go in His powerful name using His Word in this battle. We pray that through God's Word a different "fire", that of the Holy Spirit, would fall on them and they would be brought into God's kingdom!

## Biblical Truths

1. God's Word is powerful, active, and alive.
2. His Word is our offensive weapon.
3. The enemy is the devil.

## Questions

1. How well do you know God's Word? What can you do to know more?
2. What happened when you saw God's Word used against people instead of against the devil? Give examples of the impact it's had on faith, attendance at church, etc.
3. What consequences have you seen when Bible verses were cherry-picked for shortsighted purposes? What about improper or unbalanced use of law and gospel? Give examples of the impact.
4. Re-read Luther's comments. What impacted you? Why?

## Tactics

1. Study how Jesus used God's Word against the devil. Matthew 4:1-11
2. Memorize key passages: 1 John 2:14, John 6:63, John 8:31-33, Hebrews 4:12-13, Romans 8:37

## CHAPTER 13

# EMPLOYMENT OF SECRET AGENTS

*"Living agents are those who return with information."* (Sun Tzu)

God has gifted, equipped, and deployed His people in many ways. Not all are meant to be on the front lines. However, the ones on the front lines need "secret agents" supporting the efforts, providing encouragement and support to those in the thick of the battle. Prayer warriors, mentors, and trusted advisors are support teams who serve as our "spies." They can provide insight and information at key times.

Sun Tzu said, "Now the reason the enlightened prince and the wise general conquer the enemy whenever they move, and their achievements surpass those of ordinary men is foreknowledge." In the military context Sun Tzu stresses the importance of intelligence regarding the enemy. The best generals know it is critical to gain as much information on the enemy as possible prior to launching an attack. Critical information includes the location, disposition, and strength of the enemy. The enemy's morale is also important. If attacked, how hard will the enemy fight? Will the enemy flee when faced with overwhelming forces or stand its ground and fight to the death? What issues large or small is the enemy experiencing? All this data is extremely useful in helping the military general determine enemy vulnerabilities, so they can be included in the plan to achieve overall victory. The challenge, of course, is how to obtain this information.

There are several ways to gather intelligence on one's enemy. The primary way is reconnaissance. Through reconnaissance with friendly scouts, the military commander may be able to ascertain the location, disposition, and even strength of the enemy. There are other forms of intelligence in modern warfare such as signals, satellites, unmanned aerial surveillance systems to name a few. All the military intelligence collection methods feed into an intelligence estimate for the general. However, all these sophisticated reconnaissance methods are limited. They may not be sufficient to determine the more intangible but still important characteristics of the enemy–morale, internal challenges such as supply and personnel re-supply, etc. This leads to Sun Tzu's next point.

Sun Tzu said, "What is called 'foreknowledge' cannot be elicited from spirits, nor from gods, nor by analogy with past events, nor from calculations. It must be obtained from men who know the enemy situation." He states further, "Now there are five sorts of secret agents to be employed. These are native, inside, doubled, expendable, and living." In the context of this chapter, it is not necessary to delve into each of the five different types of agents Sun Tzu describes, but rather it is worth exploring the general principle in some detail using a historical example of how important the employment of "secret agents" is to achieving victory in a military campaign.

During the American Revolutionary War that took place from 1775–1783 between Great Britain and the Thirteen Original American Colonies, the colonists were at a severe disadvantage. During that time, Great Britain was overseeing the British Empire, which was the most powerful and most influential in the World. It had the largest Navy up to that time the world had ever seen. An almost equally powerful, well-trained, and disciplined expeditionary Army backed their Navy. The American Colonists had no chance at an even fight against the British. General George Washington (appointed Commander-in-Chief of the colonial army by the Continental Congress on June 15, 1775, in Philadelphia, Pennsylvania) clearly understood this, having fought as a voluntary aide-de-camp to British General Braddock during the American French and Indian War twenty years prior. Washington knew he would need to have information superiority over his foe if his Army and new Nation were going to survive. This would depend on his ability to see and understand all aspects of the British Expeditionary Army and powerful Navy operations on American littoral waters and soil. To enable these critical efforts, he established what is today known as the Culper Spy Ring.[44]

Some of the highlights of the work of this spy ring that reported directly to Washington throughout the long eight-year war included "uncovering a British counterfeiting scheme, preventing an ambush of French reinforcements, smuggling a British naval code book to Yorktown, and (most importantly) preventing Benedict Arnold from carrying out one of the greatest acts of treachery in American history: his plan to surrender West Point to the enemy." In total, each one of these efforts enabled Washington to gain an advantage over the British. When taken in totality, they allowed the young American Army just enough of an edge to achieve final victory, which led to the independence of the American Colonies.[45]

Throughout history there are numerous examples of how wartime leadership has leveraged spies to achieve victory over its foe. This has not changed in our contemporary era. Nations around the world spend billions of dollars on personnel and technology to gain the information advantage over their competitors and enemies both in military and industrial applications. Each side correctly believes this endeavor is critical to maintain a strong military defense and economy. Perhaps the following quote from Sun Tzu summarizes it best, "And therefore only the enlightened sovereign and the worthy general who can use the most intelligent people and agents are certain to achieve great things. Secret operations are essential in war; upon them the army relies on to make its every move."

There are two facets to consider when looking at this from a spiritual warfare perspective. Spies can be very useful for our side, but they are also being used by the evil one. In the book of *Numbers*, we see Moses sending out spies to the promised land.

**The Lord said to Moses, "Send some men to explore the land of Canaan, which I am giving to the Israelites. From each ancestral tribe send one of its leaders."** (Numbers 13:1-2, NIV)

His instructions were explicit and are a good example of how to use "spies."

**When Moses sent them to explore Canaan, he said, "Go up through the Negev and on into the hill country. See what the land is like and**

whether the people who live there are strong or weak, few or many. What kind of land do they live in? Is it good or bad? What kind of towns do they live in? Are they unwalled or fortified? How is the soil? Is it fertile or poor? Are there trees in it or not? Do your best to bring back some of the fruit of the land." (It was the season for the first ripe grapes.)** (Numbers 13:17-20, NIV)

These leaders came back and shared valuable information with Moses and the rest of the Israelites. Interestingly, only Joshua and Caleb recommended that they go and take possession of the land because God was with them. The others cowered in fear and came up with all the reasons not to go. The Israelites listened to the fearful ones and rebelled against God. Forty years in the desert was the consequence of not following God's will.

Two key takeaways from this. When brothers and sisters in Christ can obtain information on the evil one's activities, it is helpful in battle. But even more critical is trusting in the Lord and His strength, no matter what the spies see and hear. We know that, even though Jesus and Satan are battling against each other in this world, Jesus has won the ultimate victory and wins each day in the fight for people's souls.

Another consideration is that the evil one is adept at deploying spies. Jesus himself was on the receiving end of spy's activities.

**Keeping a close watch on him, they sent spies, who pretended to be sincere. They hoped to catch Jesus in something he said, so that they might hand him over to the power and authority of the governor.** (Luke 20:20, NIV)

But Jesus saw through it and made them look like fools. We too must be wary of spies in our midst. Scripture warns of false teachers, people in our churches who are not believers, and Satan himself masquerading.

**And no wonder, for Satan himself masquerades as an angel of light.** (2 Corinthians 11:14, NIV)

Paul mentions an incident in his letter to the Galatians. Judaizers who had infiltrated the church were requiring Gentiles to be circumcised and to obey the Law of Moses.

**This matter arose because some false believers had infiltrated our ranks to spy on the freedom we have in Christ Jesus and to make us slaves. We did not give in to them for a moment, so that the truth of the gospel might be preserved for you. (Galatians 2:4-5, NIV)

Paul and his companions did not buy into the false teaching. Instead, they were steadfast in proclaiming the truth of the gospel for all people. The truth is that salvation comes by faith in Jesus given to us by the Holy Spirit, not earned by works of the Law.

So, what does this mean for warriors in the battle? We need to depend on "spies" but be wary, too! Build your own personal "spy" network. Routinely connect with trusted advisors, prayer warriors, mentors, accountability partners. Have everyone look out for the evil one's activities and, through the discernment given by the Holy Spirit, share and plan together for the battle. Be in the Word together to discern God's truths. Watch and be wary even in Christian circles. Again, this is serious business. Lives and souls are at stake.

**I know that after I leave, savage wolves will come in among you and will not spare the flock.** (Acts 20:29, NIV)

**Watch out for false prophets. They come to you in sheep's clothing, but inwardly they are ferocious wolves.** (Matthew 7:15, NIV)

Scripture also gives us some advice on how to deal with this.

**"I am sending you out like sheep among wolves. Therefore be as shrewd as snakes and as innocent as doves.** (Matthew 10:16, NIV)

Employing "spies" is one of the many tactics needed to prepare for and achieve the best possible outcome as we face spiritual battles. We need to be careful though and not forget that our God is sovereign and has already conquered sin, death, and the devil through Jesus' sacrifice on the cross. We need not fear bad reports or overwhelming odds when we are following the supreme commander, God our Father!

**Have I not commanded you? Be strong and courageous. Do not be afraid; do not be discouraged, for the Lord your God will be with you wherever you go.** (Joshua 1:9, NIV)

## Biblical Truths

1. God is all powerful and even though it looks overwhelming at times, He prevails.

2. There are spies among us.
3. God has given us brothers and sisters for support.

**Questions**

1. What are your thoughts on "spying" on the evil one? Is it helpful or harmful and why do you believe that way?
2. What ways can you use to discern the "wolves" among you?
3. As a Jesus follower, what does being "shrewd as snakes and innocent as doves" look like?
4. Do you currently have people in your life who can help you see what's going on in the battle? How, what, and when do you communicate?

**Tactics**

1. Develop your own "spy" network. This can be people from your Advisory Staff, people you know and trust, friends, and family.
2. Be constantly watchful.
3. Continue to study and apply God's Word. Use the Bible study method found in Appendix 1.
4. Share your stories about how God has been defeating the enemy with fellow believers and "not yet" Christians.

## CHAPTER 14
# EPILOGUE

The authors hope is that this book serves as a helpful tool for the reader to use in their spiritual life. The daily grind can often be challenging and stressful with constant temptations by the evil one. We close this book with final thoughts from each of us on some of our own spiritual warfare experiences in our lives.

As I (John) stated at the beginning of the book, I served for 32 years in the United States Army and completed three 12-month combat tours of duty. My first two tours were in Iraq, and my third and final one was in Afghanistan. It is important to understand I was raised in a strong Christian household and married a Christian Woman. I always believed in a Triune God– Father, Son, and Holy Spirit– but admittedly in my early adult years, my relationship with Jesus was not my top priority.

However, there is a saying in the Army that "there are no atheists in fox holes." During my first tour in combat, which was at the beginning of the War in Iraq, I discovered the true meaning of this statement. I gave myself a fifty-fifty chance of going home to my wife and three children (at the time) in one piece. I prayed more during this time in my life than I had previously. However, I did not pray just for myself. Instead, I prayed primarily for the Soldiers I was responsible for leading in combat and for my Family back home. Indeed, I had made an uneasy peace with the fact that I may be joining Jesus in Heaven although I did not dwell on this very much at the time. The first three months of my second combat tour in Iraq were extremely difficult. One night, I became extremely sick. I am not sure if it was just a physical ailment, or my level of stress had finally overcome me physically.

Looking back now, it was probably both. However, that evening was a turning point in my spiritual life. During my physical suffering, I prayed in earnest to Jesus to help me. However, I did not have the wisdom to specify the type of help I needed, but it did not matter. Jesus knew what relief I needed, and it was not just physical. I needed spiritual aid, and after my desperate prayer He provided me immediate relief. That night Jesus was clearly with me as He always has been and always will be both in this physical life and eternity. That night I put on my spiritual armor, and I was able to effectively complete my tour of duty with spiritual energy remaining. I could not have done it without Jesus.

On my third combat tour, which was exactly one year after I completed my previous one, I was spiritually prepared. After that pivotal night in Iraq, I continued to strengthen my spiritual armor by maintaining a strong relationship with Jesus. While I was deployed to Afghanistan, I went to church as often as I could with my goal being once per week, read scripture, and received the Lord's Supper. This deployment was extremely taxing and very stressful, but with the full coat of spiritual armor I wore, I was able to get through it in good order. Once again Jesus had carried me through a very trying period in my life. The difference this time was that I had fully prepared for what I knew was coming prior to boarding the airplane that took me back into harm's way.

I still experience many trials and tribulations in my daily life as probably all who are reading this do, but what gets me through the difficult times is my relationship with the Lord Jesus. He is my Rock and keeps me grounded in what is truly important—eternal life with God.

When Gerry approached me to help him write this book, I did not hesitate. Our hope is that you not only found this book helpful but will also share it with others in your life. All of us are on the front line of spiritual warfare and need to be better prepared. Each of us must continue to fight the evil one using the tactics we have put forth throughout the book. We know without a doubt through our study of scripture, that the war is won, and that God gives us strength, boldness, and courage to continue the fight through His power.

# EPILOGUE

As John has said, our hope is that this book helps you be better prepared for the battle you are in. I (Gerry) can't stress it enough; this is a battle for people's souls that has eternal consequences. We know that in Christ, the war has been won, but the evil one has not relented and continues to bring and keep people in the darkness of their fear, sin, and death.

My journey into this realm is quite different from John's but with many parallels. I was always a scientist and mathematician at heart from my childhood. I always believed you could prove things in the material world. Equations helped us understand our world, experiments validated our ideas, and, if it couldn't, it wasn't true. As a Chemical Engineer, that's what drove my thinking and success in the corporate world. Consequently, the realm of the spiritual world never really was even a possibility in my thinking until I read a book by Frank Peretti, *This Present Darkness*. Even though I don't believe everything in this fictional book is doctrinally or theologically sound, it opened my eyes to the possibility of the spiritual realm. It sparked my interest. But career, family, and the pursuit of the Golden Ring diverted my attention away from this important area. During my corporate time, I was introduced to Sun Tzu's *The Art of War* and used it as a tool to help me succeed against our competitors. This, along with The *Book of Five Rings* by Miyamoto Musashi, became constant sources of insight and influenced my actions and thinking in significant ways. During these times however, I always thought I could discern the spiritual realm because I seemed to have a sense of the presence of evil or "spirits", but never really thought much about it until God called me to be a pastor. As I studied and experienced more, I believe the Holy Spirit opened my eyes to the possibility that not all things can be seen and not all things are explainable by science and reason. That there is a war going on in the spiritual realm beyond our ability to fully comprehend. More and more experiences seemed to reinforce this. I remember a time we were almost killed in an auto accident. A truck veered into our lane; I performed a violent swerving maneuver and to my surprise our vehicle didn't flip. I had the unmistakable feeling that an angel had kept our car from turning over. Was that true or not? I can't prove or disprove it, but it made me study angels in the bible and to my surprise, there are times angels protect God's people. Fast forward some years... as a pastor, God used me to help in a spiritual battle for a person's life. During the process I experienced health issues (vertigo, unexplained blackouts) without any physical or medical explanations. I observed human behaviors that were not of this realm, experienced the presence of darkness in the form of dark mists around our altar and was again saved from harm in a violent car accident. To our surprise, the driver of the car had the face of the devil as his profile picture. Again, was this real? I saw God's miraculous protection and healing of physical health issues for an individual and protection from suicide attempts I now believe were demonic acts of destruction. During these times in the front lines of battle, I sought help, resources, and guidance, but to my surprise, there weren't many options. The pastors I talked to didn't want to be a part of it, many resources didn't align with scripture and, in general there were very few places to go. One pastor suggested I read *The Dark Sacrament: True Stories of Modern-Day Demon Possession and Exorcism* by David Kiely and Christina McKenna which recounts true possession and harassment cases. It terrified me! Sadly, that same pastor left the ministry. I was referred to the unpublished notebook, *Immanuel Approach*, by K.D. Lehman, M.D. by someone who was constantly being brought into real life spiritual battles. This resource was probably the best source of help I found at the time. Through all of this, I realized that, as a human, I was ill prepared for the battle. The Concordia House publications, *I Am Not Afraid* and *Afraid* became great resources to help me get a clearer biblical understanding of the battle... which brings me to this book.

As I was rereading *The Art of War*, I thought it would be an interesting and helpful way to look at spiritual warfare. During this same time, God brought John into my life. This book, a practical book of tactics to help God's people be better prepared, is the rest of the story! We are by no means experts in this but have some experiences we wanted to share in the hopes it spurs you on as God's warriors. God is the ultimate source of strength, victory, and discernment. I also believe that the more people of this culture move away from Jesus, the more ground the evil one will gain, and the intensity of the warfare will increase. Brothers and sisters... I urge you to put on your armor, pick up the sword of the Spirit which is the word of God and watch how God works. You will be amazed!

And that about wraps it up. God is strong, and he wants you strong. So take everything the Master has set out for you, well-made weapons of the best materials. And put them to use so you will be able to stand up to everything the Devil throws your way. This is no weekend war that we'll walk away from and forget about in a couple of hours. This is for keeps, a life-or-death fight to the finish against the Devil and all his angels. Be prepared. You're up against far more than you can handle on your own. Take all the help you can get, every weapon God has issued, so that when it's all over but the shouting you'll still be on your feet. Truth, righteousness, peace, faith, and salvation are more than words. Learn how to apply them. You'll need them throughout your life. God's Word is an *indispensable* weapon. In the same way, prayer is essential in this ongoing warfare. Pray hard and long. Pray for your brothers and sisters. Keep your eyes open. Keep each other's spirits up so that no one falls behind or drops out. (Ephesians 6:10-18, MSG)

**Contact info:**
Website: spiritualwarfareconsulting.com
Facebook: SpiritualWarfareConsulting
Instagram: spiritual.warfare.consulting

APPENDIX 1
# BIBLE STUDY

Scripture is God's Word, and the primary means He has given us to know Him, His will, and how to live out our role individually and as the Church. It is God inspired, inerrant, and infallible– the only source of Truth. Scripture alone is used to interpret scripture. It reveals who God is, who we are, and why we are here. Luther had discovered that the word "does what it says" and "says what it does" (Bayer).

**"All Scripture is breathed out by God and profitable for teaching, for reproof, for correction, and for training in righteousness, that the messenger of God may be complete, equipped for every good work."**
(2 Timothy 3:16-17, ESV)

An important point about scripture... it is God "enfleshed." The words of scripture are both fully human and fully divine. Like other sacramental things, Christ has located himself in these words. God has given power to these words to work faith and salvation. It is "efficacious." It has the power to do what God desires.

**The words that I have spoken to you are spirit and life.** (John 6:63, ESV)

Therefore, it goes without saying that Bible study is critical to our formation and faith. It is different from devotions or the time we spend preparing to lead a study or preach. Jesus used scripture to answer those who tested him, resist temptation, find guidance, encourage His heart, comfort others, explain His actions, and ultimately face His own death.

**Reflection/Discussion Question:** How would you characterize the way you tend to read? How have your reading habits influenced the way you read scripture?

**Reflection/Discussion Question:** How has Bible study affected your life?

## Bible Study Basics

### Interpretations

The original language for the Old Testament was Hebrew and for the New Testament was Greek. The original interpretation used during Reformation times was Latin, read and spoken only by a select few. Martin Luther translated it into German so the common people could have the Word of God in their hands. The translation you use is important and there's value in reading more than one! There are basically three types of translations:

- Word-for-word (ESV- English Standard Version, NASB- New American Standard Bible, NKJV- New King James Version)
- Thought-for-thought (NIV- New International Version)
- Paraphrase (MSG- The Message, GNT- Good News Translation)

**Read and Reflect/Discuss:** 2 Timothy 3:16-17 in NIV and in MSG. Then compare it to the ESV. What differences do you see? How could these interpretations change how you understand this passage?

### Concordances

A concordance can be a powerful tool to dig deeper into a specific topic or word. Many Bibles have concordances in the back, but you can also buy concordances that are much more thorough. In your concordance, look up the word "sight" and see all the references. Many study Bibles also have background information on the people and on the specific books.

### Commentaries

To go deeper into God's Word, commentaries can be useful if they are doctrinally and theologically sound. Many study Bibles have commentaries incorporated alongside/below the texts. Remember that everything "below the line" in those Bibles are opinions! Use the same caution you would have when reading a paraphrase translation.

## Bible Apps

Bible apps like the Blue Letter Bible and Bible Gateway are powerful tools to bring these things together in one place. For instance, you can have multiple translations side-by-side, can look up specific words, and even look at the original language word/definitions (Blue Letter Bible).

The following has been attributed to Martin Luther but is unverified. It is a great illustration on Bible Study.

> **I study my Bible as I gather apples. First, I shake the whole tree that the ripest might fall. Then I shake each limb, and when I have shaken each limb, I shake each branch and every twig. Then I look under every leaf. I search the Bible as a whole like shaking the whole tree then I shake every limb-study book after book. Then I shake every branch giving attention to the chapters when they do not break the sense. Then I shake every twig, or a careful study of the paragraph and sentences and words and their meanings.**

## Key Considerations

1. God's word is for all people.
2. Scripture should always be interpreted in light of Christ and its central message of salvation through Him. Whatever scripture says relates, in some way, to Jesus and His saving work.
3. Interpretation of scripture requires prayer and humility and is ultimately not a human process but the work of the Holy Spirit through the word.

**Reflection/Discussion Questions:** What am I going to do with this? How am I going to start incorporating Bible study into my routine? Who can I ask to go along on this journey with me?

## Method for Bible Study:
## Martin Luther's Oratio, Meditatio, Tentatio

The following contains excerpts from **https://lutheranreformation.org/theology/tentatio/** Rev. Stephen Preus

Since the Word is, in fact, God speaking to us, there is no reality to be sought beyond the Word of God. Luther laid out modified steps, oratio, meditatio, tentatio, that all lead back to the Word. The first step begins with prayer for the Holy Spirit (oratio). Through meditation on God's Word (meditatio), the Spirit works. As the Spirit works, the devil attacks the Christian (tentatio). Tentatio then leads you back to God's Word.

### Oratio (true prayer)
In prayer the believer asks for understanding and steadfastness as he approaches God's Word. The very words of scripture form the language of prayer itself.

### Meditatio (study)
Meditation is simply the continual study of scripture, the very voice of God. Scripture comes with the power to both to kill and make alive.

> Possible Forms of Meditatio (Study)[47]
> **Artistic method.** Read a passage of Scripture, considering three questions as you read:
> 1. What speaks to my heart? Draw a heart beside the word that speaks to your heart.
> 2. What new thought or idea comes to me? Draw a light bulb beside the new thought or idea.
> 3. What does Scripture move me to do? Draw a hand beside the action you want to take.
>
> Consider how you can apply one of your insights today. Share your insights with a friend.
>
> **Detective method.** Read a short narrative passage from one of the Gospels. Let the story take shape in your mind's eye. Imagine the scene.

Observe all the facts. Ask the who, when, where, and what questions. Once you have the facts, interpret the facts. Ask the "why" and "for what purpose" questions. What meaning did the actions have for the characters? What meaning do the actions have for you? Then apply your study to your own life. Ask how this will change your life and what do you take away from the story?

**Treasure-Seeker method.** When reading Scripture consider the following application questions: Is there an example here for me to follow? Is there a promise to claim or a command to obey? Is there a truth to apply? Is there a prayer for me to pray? Is there sin to be confessed? Is there a question God is asking me?

**Jesus Apprentice method.** If you are unfamiliar with Scripture and don't know where to begin, choose one of the Gospels (Mark or Luke) and study to discover all you can about Jesus. Ask yourself the following questions: What seems important to Jesus? What sort of questions does He ask people? What sort of questions do people ask Him? What is Jesus inviting me to be and do?

An additional method includes written or art Journaling. The key is to find a method that helps you. When using any of these, the caution is to make sure it's "scripture interpreting scripture" not the culture or our own biases leading us away from God's Truth. Always asking what this has to say about Jesus and about salvation are good prompts.

## Tentatio (agonizing internal struggle)
When a Christian prays for the Holy Spirit and meditates on God's Word, the devil will assault with *trials, difficulties, suffering, and persecution.* The evil one resists God, hates His Word, and wants to seed doubt, misunderstanding, confusion, and contradiction. But tentatio (agonizing internal struggles) drives us back to God's Word for certainty and comfort in Jesus. He uses it as a way of turning self-seeking people back to himself.

**Group/ Partner Exercise** (Practice it together and discuss value/challenges you experienced using this method)

Oratio (2-5 minutes)
Spend a brief time in silence and pray to the Lord, through the Holy Spirit's work, to give you understanding, to open your eyes to His truths, and to give you the strength to be steadfast in His truths and diligent in study of His Word when the evil one attacks.

Meditatio (15-20 minutes)
Read: Matthew 11:28-30 in NIV and in ESV. Use one of the forms of Meditatio as you study His Word.

Tentatio (5-10 minutes)
What doubts or confusion surfaced as you read and studied this passage? Where in scripture can you go deeper to allay these?

**Individual Exercise**

Oratio- Time of silence and prayer

Meditatio- Read and study Ecclesiastes 3:1-8 in NIV and ESV. Use one of the forms of study to go deeper.

Tentatio- What questions/ words/ concepts surfaced to study or pray about further?

**Incorporating into Your Schedule**
Practice this method for 4 weeks (3 times per week) using stories from the Gospel of Luke as the focus. Share stories from the journey.

| | | |
|---|---|---|
| Luke 1:26-38 | Luke 2:22-38 | Luke 2:41-52 |
| Luke 4:1-13 | Luke 4:16-30 | Luke 4:42-44 |
| Luke 5:27-32 | Luke 6:1-5 | Luke 6:27-36 |
| Luke 7:18-23 | Luke 9:57-62 | Luke 10:1-12 |

### APPENDIX 2
# PRAYER GUIDE

**Rejoice always, pray without ceasing, give thanks in all circumstances; for this is the will of God in Christ Jesus for you.**

(1 Thessalonians 5:16-18, ESV)

## Reflect

Quiet yourself. Consider sitting in silence for two minutes. Read and reflect on the following passages.

**Continue steadfastly in prayer, being watchful in it with thanksgiving.**

(Colossians 4:2, ESV)

**...pray without ceasing** (1 Thessalonians 5:17, ESV)

**O you who hear prayer, to you shall all flesh come.** (Psalm 65:2, ESV)

## Pray Using "ACTS" Model

### Adoration

Think about and thank God for who He is. Consider His creation, your life and blessings, and your salvation in Christ.

### Confession

Confess your sins to God. Repent (turn away from) all things that hurt your walk with God and your faith.

**If we confess our sins, he is faithful and just to forgive us our sins and to cleanse us from all unrighteousness.** (1 John 1:9 ESV)

## Thanksgiving
Thank God for all things in your life, including your enemies, trials, and challenges.

## Supplication
Pray for:
1. People you have promised to pray for and/or been led by the Holy Spirit to pray for
2. The Church and its mission
   - Financial and people resources
   - Unity in ministry–local, district and synod
   - Reaching the pre-Christians
   - Caring and loving the homeless and hungry
   - Truth in proclamation and teaching
   - Boldness, courage, and strength to follow God's lead
   - Missionaries
   - Military Chaplains
   - Pastors, staff, and teachers
3. World, Nation, and Community
   - Wisdom and discernment for leaders
   - Truth and justice
   - Peace
   - Global problems–hunger, trafficking, orphans, etc.
   - Blessings on industry and commerce
   - Agriculture
4. Baptismal Life for Jesus Followers
   - Protection from the evil one
   - Faith, hope, and love
   - Divine Guidance
   - For the Holy Spirit's guidance and strength
   - Willingness and joy in using gifts
   - Guidance in calling

- Proper use of wealth and leisure
- Right knowledge of God
- Reconciliation
- Aid against temptation
- Purity, humility, and patience
5. Home and Family
    - Marriages
    - Children
    - Teenagers and young adults
    - Finances
6. Times of Need
    - Sickness
    - Death
    - Mourning
    - Affliction and distress
    - Loneliness
    - Disability
    - Unemployed
    - Time of disaster
7. Times of Joy
    - Restoration of health
    - Birth of a child
    - Birthday
    - Anniversary
    - Graduations
8. Other areas of Prayer

## Morning and Evening Prayers

### Morning Prayer
*In the morning when you first get up, remind yourself of your identity in Him and pray this prayer.*
Thank you for protecting me through the night and for giving me rest. Be with me this day. Give your angels charge over me to protect me from

the evil one. Give me strength to resist temptations and keep me from sin and all evil. Help me to be faithful and do your will in all that I do today. I commend my mind, body, soul, and everything into your hands. It's in you alone I have life and salvation. Thank you for choosing me to be your beloved child. I pray this in Jesus' name. Amen

*Then sing your favorite praise song or hymn, study God's Word or complete a devotion, recite the Apostle's Creed, put on your spiritual armor, and then enter the battle with joy and confidence knowing He is with you.*

**Evening Prayer**
*When you go to bed, pray this prayer.*

Thank you for bringing me safely through this day and for providing all my needs. Forgive me for all the sins I committed today and help me to do better tomorrow. Please watch over me as I sleep. Give your angels charge over me to protect me from the evil one. It's into your nail scarred hands I commit everything—my mind, body, and soul. You are my fortress, my refuge and it's in you I have life and salvation. Thank you for choosing me as your child. I pray all these things in your Son's name... in the name of Jesus who taught us to pray:

> Our Father, who art in heaven, hallowed be thy name, thy Kingdom come, thy will be done on earth as it is in heaven. Give us this day our daily bread and forgive us our sins as we forgive those who sin against us. Lead us not into temptation but deliver us from evil. For thine is the kingdom and the power and the glory, forever and ever. AMEN

*Then go to sleep in His peace.*

APPENDIX 3

# WORD STUDIES

**Word Study- Satan, Devil**

Read the following passages and note the devil's origin and what originates in him.

Genesis 3:7
Isaiah 14:12-20
Ezekiel 28:14-19
John 8:44
Revelation 12:7-9

Did anything surprise you? What and why?

_____
_____

Read the following passages and record the names and titles associated with the evil one.

Genesis 3:4
Matthew 12:24; 13:19
Luke 10:18
John 8:44; 14:30
Ephesians 2:2; 6:12
2 Corinthians 4:4; 6:15
1 Peter 5:8
Revelation 9:11; 12:10; 20:2

What insight do these give you into who the evil one is and what he uses in the battle for souls?
_____
_____

Read the following passages to understand what he is trying to do.
- Job 2:4,5
- Mark 4:15
- Luke 4:6-8
- John 13:2,27
- 2 Thessalonians 2:3,4

What are his goals?
_____
_____

What is his character and how is he trying to accomplish this? Read the following passages and note his tools.
- Genesis 3:1
- Job 1:9
- Matthew 4:6
- Luke 8:29; 13:16
- John 8:44
- 2 Corinthians 2:11; 11:3, 14
- Ephesians 2:2
- 1 Timothy 3:6
- James 4:7
- 1 John 2:13
- 1 Peter 5:9
- Revelation 12:9

What are the tools he has most effectively used on you?
_____
_____

Read the following passages to discover the tactics he uses.
Job 2:7
1 Chronicles 21:1
Zechariah 3:1
Luke 22:31
2 Corinthians 11:3, 14, 15

Which tactics have you seen used the most?
_____
_____

There is judgment upon the devil. Christ has triumphed over him. Read the good news in the following passages.
Genesis 3:15
Matthew 4:1-11; 25:41
Mark 3:27, 28
Luke 10:18
John 12:31; 16:11
Romans 16:20

Christ has defeated the devil. The deceiver, the evil one, faces God's judgment. How does this good news affect your faith walk and your ability to be the warrior God has called you to be?
_____
_____

The believer has power over temptation, sin, and the devil.
2 Corinthians 2:11
Ephesians 6:11-16
James 4:7
1 Peter 5:9
1 John 2:13
Revelation 12:10,11

You have God-given strength and power to resist. How are you going to increase your readiness for the war you are in?
_____
_____

**Word Study- demons**

Read the following passages describing their nature.
- Matthew 10:1, 12:24-30
- Mark 5:8-9
- Luke 8:29; 10:17,18

Who are they working for and why is that important to understand?
_____
_____

They have numerous abilities that scripture captures. Read the following and note what they can do.
- Matthew 4:24; 8:29-33
- Mark 1:23-24, 32; 5:1-5
- Acts 19:13-16
- 1 Corinthians 10:20
- 1 Timothy 4:1

What insight does this give you?
_____
_____

There are many instances of demon oppression and possession recorded in scripture. Read the following to learn more about the symptoms, consequences, and Jesus' power over demonic influence.
- Matthew 8:28-34; 9:32-33; 12:22-23; 15:22-28; 17:14-21
- Mark 1:23-26; 16:9
- What did you learn?

_____
_____

APPENDIX 4

# ADVISORY STAFF Q&A

**1. What is an Advisory Staff?**
It is a sounding board, think tank, advisory group, etc. to support the leader.

**2. How often does it meet?**
Once per month with communication between meetings.

**3. Is there a specific agenda and, if so, what does it include?**
The agenda is set by the leader. The agenda always includes a time to check in with each other, pray for, and care for each other. There is also time to discuss any areas the leader needs counsel and support.

**4. What topics do you discuss?**
Job, personal issues (health, marriage, family, etc.), life goals, personal finances, temptations, spiritual challenges, and anything else in life that needs to be discussed. The Wholeness Wheel is a good guide to discern possible areas needing attention. It is never simply the leader reporting on what they had done or were going to do. It is driven by questions, inquiry, struggle, perspective, etc.

At the end of the time together, there is always actions steps determined by the group. Sometimes the action steps are just the leaders. Other times it includes a subset of the group.

**5. Do you ever read a book together related to the topics?**
Yes, depending on what is going on. You can also discuss articles or current cultural trends.

**6. How do you pick the members of the Advisory Staff, how many are on it, and what do you ask of them for a commitment?**
The leader picks 5–7 staff members. These are people who you trust and respect. They have an interest in your growth. These people can be transparent and engage in whatever you need to discuss. They need to have a strong and growing faith. The commitments include confidentiality and honesty, a willingness to tell you if a thought or idea was a bad one, and to faithfully attend the meetings. The agreement is to share the truth in love. Since this is relationship based, there is no time limit to participating. The standing rule is:

*"You can ask me anything you want about my life. I will answer you as honestly as I can. I get to ask you about your life, and your honesty is also required."*

Your staff should include the following "voices:"
- Prophet: Brings truth into your life. They will challenge you to look at how you are living and speak truth into that.
- Cheerleader: Gives you unabashed, enthusiastic, unconditional acceptance no matter what.
- Harasser: Helps you laugh at yourself and not take life too seriously. They help you maintain and regain perspective.
- Guide: They don't take everything at face value and look for the nuances to help you discover the beliefs and outside influences that unconsciously guide you.

**7. What is your commitment to them?**
To be concerned about their development.... how they might grow by being a part of the staff. It is a two-way deal, and ones who participated shared that they have grown as husbands, fathers, leaders, and managers.

# SOURCES

The following is the list of major sources we used in writing this book. Regarding the military vignettes: I (John) have studied these vignettes by reading numerous books and watching countless documentaries while serving in the U.S. Army over 32 years, so I am intimately familiar with them. In several cases, I had the good fortune to visit some of the historical sites like Gettysburg and Little Big Horn battlefields. If there is no page number associated with the citation, it is because I provide a single reference if the reader wishes to learn more about a particular historical battle. Keep in mind, there are multiple sources available for all these historical vignettes. While writing this book, I (John) used Google Search and Wikipedia extensively to verify historical battlefield locations, dates of the battles, and casualty figures. I (Gerry) provided several additional Spiritual references that the reader may find helpful that were not specifically referenced in the book.

## Works Cited and Referenced

Robert H. Bennett, I am Not Afraid: Demon Possession and Spiritual Warfare (Saint Louis: Concordia Publishing House, 2013), 141.

Robert H. Bennett, I am Not Afraid: Demon Possession and Spiritual Warfare (Saint Louis: Concordia Publishing House, 2013), 141.

Robert H. Bennett, I am Not Afraid: Demon Possession and Spiritual Warfare (Saint Louis: Concordia Publishing House, 2013), 137.

Robert H. Bennett, I am Not Afraid: Demon Possession and Spiritual Warfare (Saint Louis: Concordia Publishing House, 2013), 117.

Jeffrey A. Gibbs, Concordia Commentary - Matthew 1:1-11:1: A Theological Exposition of Sacred Scripture (Saint Louis: Concordia Publishing House: 2006), 453.

All references from Sun Tzu that the authors used in this book were taken directly from The Art of War by Sun Tzu, translated with an introduction by Samuel B. Griffith with a Foreword by L.H. Liddell Hart; Oxford University Press, London, 1963. The references are attributed to Sun Tzu followed by quotations. The quotations that precede each chapter are also taken directly from The Art of War.

U.S. Army, ADP 3-0 Operations (Washington D.C.: Headquarters, Department of the Army, 2019), 53.

U.S. Army, ADP 3-0 Operations (Washington D.C.: Headquarters, Department of the Army, 2019), 53.

U.S. Army, ADP 3-90 Offense and Defense (Washington D.C.: Headquarters, Department of the Army, 2019), 48.

U.S. Army, ADP 3-90 Offense and Defense (Washington D.C.: Headquarters, Department of the Army, 2019), 48.

U.S. Army, FM 5-0 Planning and Orders Production, (Washington D.C.: Headquarters, Department of the Army, 2022), 187.

Clifford J. Rogers ed., TY Seidule ed., Samuel J. Watson ed., The West Point History of the Civil War. (New York: Simon and Schuster: 2014).

Geoffrey C. Ward, The Vietnam War: An Intimate History. (New York: Penguin Random House LLC, 2017).

David R. Palmer, Summons of the Trumpet (Novato, CA: Presidio Press, 1978).

Bill O'Reilly and Martin Dugard, Killing England: A Brutal Struggle for American Independence (New York: Henry Holt and Company, 2017).

Steven P. Mueller, Called to Believe, Teach, and Confess: An Introduction to Doctrinal Theology (Eugene, Oregon: Wipf & Stock, 2005), 201.

Carl Von Clausewitz, Edited and Translated by Michael Howard and Peter Paret, On War (Princeton, New Jersey: Princeton University, 1976), 703.

David R. Palmer, Summons of the Trumpet (Novato, CA: Presidio Press, 1978). (Palmer, 1978).

Copyright 1997 InterLutheran Coordinating Committee on Ministerial Health and Wellness of the Evangelical Lutheran Church in America and the Lutheran Church–Missouri Synod.

Stephen W. Smith and Peter M. Ivey, Solo: Creating Space with God (Coppell, Texas: Made in the USA, 2021).

# SOURCES

U.S. Army, ADP 3-90 Offense and Defense (Washington D.C.: Headquarters, Department of the Army, 2019), 49.

U.S. Army, ADP 3-90 Offense and Defense (Washington D.C.: Headquarters, Department of the Army, 2019), 19.

Clifford J. Rogers ed., TY Seidule ed., Samuel J. Watson ed., The West Point History of World War II: Volume 1. New York: Simon and Schuster: 2015).

Allan R. Millett, Peter Maslowski, and William B. Feis P. M., For the Common Defense: A Military History of the United States from 1607 to 2012 (New York: Simon and Schuster, 2012).

Allan R. Millett, Peter Maslowski, and William B. Feis P. M., For the Common Defense: A Military History of the United States from 1607 to 2012 (New York: Simon and Schuster, 2012).

Clifford J. Rogers ed., TY Seidule ed., Samuel J. Watson ed., The West Point History of the Civil War. New York: Simon and Schuster: 2014).

Weimar edition 45,709f- Erlangen Edition Rvsd 2nd Addition 49, 358 - Revised Halle or Walch edition published in St. Louis), 8,576.

Leo Barron, High Tide in the Korean War (Mechanicsburg, PA: Stackpole Books, 2015).

Martin Luther, Weimer edition of Luther's Letters, Briefe. edition published at St

Louis 10, 1756: 10, 239-German Section Erlanger edition revised 2nd edition 56, 45-Revised Halle or Walch.

U.S. Army, FM 3-0 Operations (Washington D.C.: Headquarters, Department of the Army, 2022), A-3.

T.R. Fehrenbach, T., This Kind of War: The Classic Military History of the Korean War (New York: Macmillan, 1963).

Geoffrey Parker ed., The Cambridge History of Warfare, 2nd Edition (Cambridge University Printing House, 2020).

U.S. Army, FM 5-0 Planning and Orders Production (Washington D.C.: Headquarters, Department of the Army, 2022), 114.

Clifford J. Rogers ed., TY Seidule ed., Samuel J. Watson ed., The West Point History of the American Revolution (New York: Simon and Schuster: 2017).

Nathaniel Philbrick, The Last Stand: Custer, Sitting Bull, and the battle of Little Bighorn. New York: Penguin Group, 2010).

Chris Carey, Great Battles: Thermopylae. (New York: Oxford University Press, 2019).

U.S. Army, FM 5-0 Planning and Orders Production (Washington D.C.: Headquarters, Department of the Army, 2022), 114.

Charles Rivers Editors, Rome's Most Notorious Defeats: The History and Legacy of the Battle of Cannae and the Battle of the Teutoburg Forest (Digital Publication: Charles River Editors, 2016).

Clifford J. Rogers ed., TY Seidule ed., Samuel J. Watson ed., The West Point History of World War II: Volume 1. (New York: Simon and Schuster: 2015).

LT. Gen. Harold G. Moore (Ret.) and Joseph L. Galloway, Galloway, We Were Soldiers Once...And Young. (New York: Random House, 1992).

U.S. Army, FM 3-0 Operations (Washington D.C.: Headquarters, Department of the Army, 2022), A-3. Hourly History, The Battle of Iwo Jima (Digital Publication: Hourly History, 2020).

E. Plass, What Luther Says: A Practical In-Home Anthology for the Active Christian (Saint Louis: Concordia Publishing House, 1959), 4746.

Bill O'Reilly and Martin Dugard, Killing England: A Brutal Struggle for American Independence (New York: Henry Holt and Company, 2017).

Brian Kilmeade and Don Yaeger, George Washington's Secret Six: A Spy Ring that Saved the American Revolution. (New York: Penguin Group, 2013).

[46] Karl D. Lehman, M.D., The Immanuel Approach (to Emotional Healing and to Life) (Copyright 2013), Draft.

## Additional Helpful Resources

Robert H. Bennett, Afraid: Demon Possession and Spiritual Warfare in America (Saint Louis: Concordia Publishing House, 2016).

Adele A. Calhoun, Spiritual Disciplines Handbook: Practices That Transform Us (Illinois: IVP Books, Downers Grove, 2015).

John D. Eckrich M.D., Vocation and Wellness (Digital Publication: Tenth Power Publishing, 2016).

Richard J. Foster, Celebration of Discipline: The Path to Spiritual Growth, (San Francisco: Harper: 1978, 1988, 1998).

Christopher M. Kennedy, Equipped: The Armor of God for Everyday Struggles, (Saint Louis: Concordia Publishing House [Luther, Weimer edition of Luther's Letters, Briefe, 1756]).

John W. Kleinig, Grace Upon Grace: Spirituality for Today (Saint Louis: Concordia Publishing House, 2008).

Martin Luther, M., Luther's Small Catechism with Explanation (Saint Louis: Concordia Publishing House, 2019).

R. Wicks, Bounce: Living the Resilient Life (New York: Oxford University Press, 2010).

Darrell Zimmerman, Reclaiming the Joy of Ministry (Produced with the assistance of Tenth Power Publishing, 2020).

# ABOUT THE AUTHORS

**Gerry Harrow** is currently serving as a Pastor in his local church. Prior to his Ministry, he served in various corporations for several years. He and his Wife live in Central Texas.

**John Leffers** is a retired U.S. Army officer who has a passion for military history and is actively involved in his church and community. He and his Wife live in Central Texas.

For more information about the authors, their professional services, or to learn about available workshops, visit www.spiritualwarfareconsulting.com.

This book is available in paperback and e-book format. For more information on the book, visit the publisher at www.tenthpowerpublishing.com.

SPIRITUAL WARFARE
CONSULTING

# ENDNOTES

1 Robert H. Bennett, *I am Not Afraid: Demon Possession and Spiritual Warfare* (Saint Louis: Concordia Publishing House, 2013), 141.

2 Robert H. Bennett, *I am Not Afraid: Demon Possession and Spiritual Warfare* (Saint Louis: Concordia Publishing House, 2013), 141.

3 Robert H. Bennett, *I am Not Afraid: Demon Possession and Spiritual Warfare* (Saint Louis: Concordia Publishing House, 2013), 137.

4 Robert H. Bennett, *I am Not Afraid: Demon Possession and Spiritual Warfare* (Saint Louis: Concordia Publishing House, 2013), 117.

5 Jeffrey A. Gibbs, *Concordia Commentary - Matthew 1:1-11:1: A Theological Exposition of Sacred Scripture* (Saint Louis: Concordia Publishing House: 2006), 453.

6 All references from Sun Tzu that the authors used in this book were taken directly from *The Art of War* by Sun Tzu, translated with an introduction by Samuel B. Griffith with a Foreword by L.H. Liddell Hart; Oxford University Press, London, 1963. The references are attributed to Sun Tzu followed by quotations. The quotations that precede each chapter are also taken directly from *The Art of War*.

7 U.S. Army, *ADP 3-0 Operations* (Washington D.C.: Headquarters, Department of the Army, 2019), 53.

8 U.S. Army, *ADP 3-0 Operations* (Washington D.C.: Headquarters, Department of the Army, 2019), 53.

**9** U.S. Army, *ADP 3-90 Offense and Defense* (Washington D.C.: Headquarters, Department of the Army, 2019), 48.

**10** U.S. Army, *ADP 3-90 Offense and Defense* (Washington D.C.: Headquarters, Department of the Army, 2019), 48.

**11** U.S. Army, *FM 5-0 Planning and Orders Production*, (Washington D.C.: Headquarters, Department of the Army, 2022), 187.

**12** Clifford J. Rogers ed., TY Seidule ed., Samuel J. Watson ed., *The West Point History of the Civil War.* (New York: Simon and Schuster: 2014).

**13** Geoffrey C. Ward, *The Vietnam War: An Intimate History.* (New York: Penguin Random House LLC, 2017).

**14** David R. Palmer, *Summons of the Trumpet* (Novato, CA: Presidio Press, 1978).

**15** Bill O'Reilly and Martin Dugard, *Killing England: A Brutal Struggle for American Independence* (New York: Henry Holt and Company, 2017).

**16** Steven P. Mueller, *Called to Believe, Teach, and Confess: An Introduction to Doctrinal Theology* (Eugene, Oregon: Wipf & Stock, 2005), 201.

**17** Carl Von Clausewitz, Edited and Translated by Michael Howard and Peter Paret, *On War* (Princeton, New Jersey: Princeton University, 1976), 703.

**18** David R. Palmer, *Summons of the Trumpet* (Novato, CA: Presidio Press, 1978). (Palmer, 1978).

**19** Copyright 1997 InterLutheran Coordinating Committee on Ministerial Health and Wellness of the Evangelical Lutheran Church in America and the Lutheran Church–Missouri Synod.

**20** Stephen W. Smith and Peter M. Ivey, *Solo: Creating Space with God* (Coppell, Texas: Made in the USA, 2021).

**21** U.S. Army, *ADP 3-90 Offense and Defense* (Washington D.C.: Headquarters, Department of the Army, 2019), 49.

22 U.S. Army, *ADP 3-90 Offense and Defense* (Washington D.C.: Headquarters, Department of the Army, 2019), 19.

23 Clifford J. Rogers ed., TY Seidule ed., Samuel J. Watson ed., *The West Point History of World War II: Volume 1.* New York: Simon and Schuster: 2015).

24 Allan R. Millett, Peter Maslowski, and William B. Feis P. M., *For the Common Defense: A Military History of the United States from 1607 to 2012* (New York: Simon and Schuster, 2012).

25 Allan R. Millett, Peter Maslowski, and William B. Feis P. M., *For the Common Defense: A Military History of the United States from 1607 to 2012* (New York: Simon and Schuster, 2012).

26 Clifford J. Rogers ed., TY Seidule ed., Samuel J. Watson ed., *The West Point History of the Civil War.* New York: Simon and Schuster: 2014).

27 Weimar edition 45,709f- Erlangen Edition Rvsd 2nd Addition 49, 358 - Revised Halle or Walch edition published in St. Louis), 8,576.

28 Leo Barron, *High Tide in the Korean War* (Mechanicsburg, PA: Stackpole Books, 2015).

29 Martin Luther, *Weimer edition of Luther's Letters, Briefe.* edition published at St Louis 10, 1756: 10, 239-German Section Erlanger edition revised 2nd edition 56, 45-Revised Halle or Walch.

30 U.S. Army, *FM 3-0 Operations* (Washington D.C.: Headquarters, Department of the Army, 2022), A-3.

31 T.R. Fehrenbach, T., *This Kind of War: The Classic Military History of the Korean War* (New York: Macmillan, 1963).

32 Geoffrey Parker ed., *The Cambridge History of Warfare, 2nd Edition* (Cambridge University Printing House, 2020).

33 U.S. Army, FM 5-0 Planning and Orders Production (Washington D.C.: Headquarters, Department of the Army, 2022), 114.

34 Clifford J. Rogers ed., TY Seidule ed., Samuel J. Watson ed., *The West Point History of the American Revolution* (New York: Simon and Schuster: 2017).

**35** Nathaniel Philbrick, The Last Stand: Custer, Sitting Bull, and the battle of Little Bighorn. New York: Penguin Group, 2010).

**36** Chris Carey, *Great Battles: Thermopylae.* (New York: Oxford University Press, 2019).

**37** U.S. Army, *FM 5-0 Planning and Orders Production* (Washington D.C.: Headquarters, Department of the Army, 2022), 114.

**38** Charles Rivers Editors, *Rome's Most Notorious Defeats: The History and Legacy of the Battle of Cannae and the Battle of the Teutoburg Forest* (Digital Publication: Charles River Editors, 2016).

**39** Clifford J. Rogers ed., TY Seidule ed., Samuel J. Watson ed., *The West Point History of World War II: Volume 1.* (New York: Simon and Schuster: 2015).

**40** LT. Gen. Harold G. Moore (Ret.) and Joseph L. Galloway, Galloway, *We Were Soldiers Once...And Young.* (New York: Random House, 1992).

**41** U.S. Army, *FM 3-0 Operations* (Washington D.C.: Headquarters, Department of the Army, 2022), A-3.

**42** Hourly History, *The Battle of Iwo Jima* (Digital Publication: Hourly History, 2020).

**43** E. Plass, *What Luther Says: A Practical In-Home Anthology for the Active Christian* (Saint Louis: Concordia Publishing House, 1959), 4746.

**44** Bill O'Reilly and Martin Dugard, *Killing England: A Brutal Struggle for American Independence* (New York: Henry Holt and Company, 2017).

**45** Brian Kilmeade and Don Yaeger, *George Washington's Secret Six: A Spy Ring that Saved the American Revolution.* (New York: Penguin Group, 2013).

**46** Karl D. Lehman, M.D., *The Immanuel Approach (to Emotional Healing and to Life)* (Copyright 2013), Draft.

**47** Taken from *Spiritual Disciplines Handbook*, by Adele Ahlberg Calhoun

Made in the USA
Middletown, DE
20 April 2023

29119417R00089